AF610127

austro-hungarian pianists

lili kraus

friedrich gulda

ingrid haebler

discographies compiled by john hunt

Austro-Hungarian Pianists
Discographies
Lili Kraus, Friedrich Gulda, Ingrid Haebler

John Hunt

ISBN 978-1-901395-29-7

Travis & Emery Music Bookshop
17 Cecil Court
London
WC2N 4EZ
United Kingdom.
Tel. (+44) (0) 20 7240 2129.
newpublications@travis-and-emery.com

Contents

Austro-Hungarian pianists: an introduction

In this very personal choice of remarkable pianists, which features names possibly less well-known to younger record collectors, Lili Kraus (1903-1986) came from the era when the old Austro-Hungarian Empire and its artistic traditions still held sway. However, Friedrich Gulda (1930-2000) and Ingrid Haebler (born 1929) began their training when the old empire had ceased to exist, although the musical traditions of Vienna and its environs still retained their old values and influences.

Despite the fact that all three recorded extensively, their respective legacies are nowadays less widely appreciated. In the case of Lili Kraus, this was partly due to the political upheavals of World War II (described below by Frans Schreuder). In Gulda's case it was his improvisatory and jazz-influenced style which may have alienated some diehard followers of classical pianism. Ingrid Haebler seems, in my view, to have been the victim of pure prejudice, dismissed by some as too Viennese or "gemütlich" in her piano style (I would characterise her as possessing refinement and integrity in equal measure).

I am indebted to Yasushi Aisa, John Baker, Michael Gray, John Hancock, Detlef Kissmann, Roderick Krüsemann, Ruth Pope and Frans Schreuder for assistance and stimulation in the preparation of these discographies. Michael Gray brought to my attention correspondence between the management of Vienna's Konzerthaus and Otto Preiser, at the time involved with recordings for the old Haydn Society label: this indicates that during the early 1950s Lili Kraus undertook a not inconsiderable but unspecified programme of recordings of works by Haydn, Schubert and Chopin which have never seen the light of day. Detlef Kissmann very helpfully brought to my attention a compilation devoted to Friedrich Gulda with special emphasis on his jazz career (*Wanderer zwischen Welten* was published by Bibliothek der Provinz in 2005).

John Hunt 2014

Remembering Lili Kraus: a vanishing tradition

On 6 November 1986, at the age of 83, died one of the great artists of our time and one of EPTA's most eminent patrons – Madame Lili Kraus. She once wrote to me: "EPTA is certainly one of the civilised musical endeavours and achievements of our time; it commands respect and gratitude". In 1982 severe arthritis brought an end to her concert career, an eventful life, spanning over 50 years of concerts, recordings, teaching and lecturing.

Lili Kraus was of Hungarian descent but had British nationality and, after residing in several countries, she settled for a while in London. In 1966 she went to the United States where she lived until her death in 1986. There she was Artist-in-Residence at Texas Christian University and was a permanent member of the jury at the prestigious Van Cliburn Competition.

World War II brought a dramatic disruption to her life. In 1940 she had left Europe for a world tour, via the Pacific, which was to culminate with her American debut in 1943. But fate arranged it differently. She was travelling with her husband, their two children and with Szymon Goldberg, the violinist with whom she had formed a famous Duo while living in Vienna. In 1942 they were trapped in the Dutch Indies (now Indonesia) by the Japanese invasion and forced to remain there for three and a half years. Lili Kraus, classified as a 'foreigner' was not considered an 'enemy of the state' and she was allowed to give concerts in various camps where the Dutch were interned.
I was also among the internees, and I vividly recall a recital given by Lili when I was only twelve years old. I still have in front of my eyes that beautiful pianist with an extraordinary charisma. We met again after the war and we became close friends, wrote regularly to one another and our correspondence has has now been brought to an end by her death. I shall always treasure her generous comments: "It is not only the fact that you heard me in the camp but rather the quality of your listening that created our relationship, as is the quality of your being that made me respond to you the way I did".

Lili helped many internees not only through her inspiring performances but also by smuggling letters and money from one camp to another. Eventually she was betrayed and arrested as a 'collaborator' by the *Kempei Tai* (the equivalent of the Gestapo). Hunger, arduous physical work and much mental strain were her lot but she was philosophical about it and did everything in her power to keep her spirit: "I had to fall back wholly on myself. During the period without the instrument and music, my attitude to music became much more profound and spiritual. I went repeatedly over my repertoire and technique mentally, finding new wonders I had not even thought of before. When I finally got a piano I discovered that there was no limit to memory, technique and vision". And strangely enough: "All the forced manual labour strengthened my hands and fingers miraculously, and afterwards I found that I could handle the piano with greater ease than before".

However, as with all traumatic experiences, the effects are experienced only later. She was freed in 1945 at the end of the war and went to Australia where she found herself forced to give many concerts as she was the only breadwinner of the family. Later on her European tours resumed, but it became obvious that her playing had considerably lost its exquisite qualities. The foundation under that exuberant, impulsive temperament in perpetual search for beauty, had been weakened and the strain of the internment and of the aftermath had brought an imbalance in her performance and she even developed memory slips. She wrote: "It was the worst Hungarian playing ever heard, awful and undisciplined". But she was very determined to recapture her way of playing which had helped to build her international reputation. She spent several years working with an iron will and great discipline, remembering how she managed during those terrible years as a prisoner when her mental studies had sustained her spirit and helped her grow as an artist. She took up Yoga exercises and

and relaxation disciplines and she succeeded in regaining her name among the great artists, as a fine interpreter of Chopin and Beethoven and particularly of Haydn, Mozart, Bartok, to Schubert. Her special gifts stemmed from her highly developed musical intelligence and a strong intuition of the spiritual message 'between the notes'. Like other exceptionally gifted persons, she had many other talents and interests. She was adept at drawing and painting, studied comparative philosophy and religion, and was a fervent mountain climber and animal lover ("there is no end to what men can learn from animals"). Human contact was, however, most important for Lili.

As a child she had been more attracted to ballet and the violin than to the piano, but when she auditioned for the Budapest Royal Music Academy, at the age of eight, she was accepted to study piano. She had lessons only for about two years before entering the Academy. "I hated the piano until I discovered that I could improvise and play every tune by ear, with my own accompaniment". Among her teachers were Kodaly for theory and Bartok for piano. Lili learned much from Bartok's enormous knowledge of the classics (his special love was Brahms) and of course became thoroughly acquainted with Bartok's own works and their idiomatic performances. Thorough knowledge of the original folk songs and dances was essential: "When playing Bartok's arrangements I cannot help singing the words to myself, and of course the very metrum of the text is also the rhythm of the music. In Hungary, where the very text of our language defines the phrasing of our music, the accent is always on the first syllable. Only when you know the character of the text are you able to play the syncopated notes of the text clearly". I heard her give, during a recital, a most enlightening and amusing explanation of the 15 Hungarian *Peasant Songs*. Many music lovers before World War II made their first acquaintance with Bartok's piano music through Lili's concerts and records. She was the first pianist, apart from the composer himself, to record some of his works at his request. Moreover, one of the last records she made was devoted entirely to Bartok.

At the end of the last century, the most influential schools of pianistic thought (derived from Beethoven, through Czerny) in Central Europe were those of Liszt and Leschetizky. After Liszt-orientated Budapest, Lili Kraus studied in Vienna with the legendary Leschetizky-pupil and Beethoven interpreter Artur Schnabel. She became one of his favourite pupils, especially because of her 'Spielfreudigkeit'. For a time she was one of his assistants, and later on he called her his 'musical heiress'. Whilst maintaining her resolutely independent character, she was strongly influenced by these two greats, Schnabel and Bartok. "Schnabel's first and last concern was the music itself, through the medium of the piano. To achieve through intense study a free 'con amore' and a totally alive delivery remained his principal preoccupation". Schnabel's motto was "Safety last" and Lili later said it in her inimitable way: "Only fools can expect mere perfection from other fools". She continued Schnabel's pioneering work in introducing Mozart and Schubert to the audiences and has recorded the so-called Schubert "Grazer Fantasie", discovered in 1969. She was one of the daring pianists to devote entire programmes to Haydn and, while in Vienna, the well-known Eduard Steuermann encouraged her to play some contemporary music. Thus the music of Stravinsky or Debussy was quite often included in her recitals.

Lili Kraus started to teach when she was only eight years old and she was just over twenty when she was invited to join the staff of the Vienna Music Academy. Her *Master Classes* became known as important cultural events after the war. She was usually gentle, stimulating and inspiring. However, if a student was too preoccupied with himself or the instrument, she could be intolerant, even asking why that student bothered to play the piano. Or she would advise a thorough study of the text "for the composer was also musical!" Fortunately two recordings still exist of her teaching. In her delightful Hungarian-accented English, countless observations and metaphors go to the heart of myriad musical and pianistic problems. In the early 50s she did pioneer work for all piano students in recording the easy repertoire which one never hears in concert halls.

She recorded all the Mozart concertos and sonatas which she performed in New York City during the 1966-67 and 1967-68 seasons. Her Mozart playing reflected an ideal blend of increasingly rare individualism of past generations and musicological insights of more recent years, having studied in depth the possibilities of the Hammerklavier. All the facets of Mozart's genius were revealed by her, including the dramatic element (especially in the later works) so often ignored by other pianists. To sample Lili Kraus' unequalled understanding of Mozart, one should read a detailed report of one of the Mozart courses she gave in the USA or the introduction to the book of cadenzas she wrote for the concertos.

The *Sturm und Drang* of Beethoven, the balance of melancholy and dance elements in Schubert, an exciting contrast between the Eusebius and Florestan poles of Schumann's output, and the broodiness of Brahms, all these were vividly brought to life in her performances. So many of these characteristics have virtually vanished in all too predictable playing one usually hears today. Lili once remarked: "The contemporary output of pianists is, but for a few exceptions, cut off from the great traditions", adding "I was born in an age when you could not derive your musical interpretations from gramophone records; your own imagination, vision and artistic will had to shape what you played". However she did advise her students to listen especially to historic recordings of the past greats. Among those chosen few, she will take her place.

Frans Schreuder 1987

This article first appeared in the journal of the European Piano Teachers' Association, translated by Michael Davidson, and is reproduced here with permission.

JOHANN SEBASTIAN BACH (1685-1750)

chromatic fantasy and fugue in d minor BWV 903

televised by radio canada montreal on 31 january 1961
dvd: video artists international 4359

recorded in the vanguard studios new york city
lp: vanguard VA 25003
cd: vanguard VBD 25003

a bach miscellany: bourree in e minor from suite BWV 996; capriccio on the departure of a beloved brother BWV 992; gavotte and musette from english suite BWV 808; little prelude in c minor BWV 899; little prelude in c BWV 924; little prelude in f BWV 927; little prelude in c BWV 939; little prelude in c minor BWV 934; little prelude in c BWV 933; march in d BWVanh 122; march in e flat BWVanh 127; minuet in g BWVanh 114; minuet in g from overture BWV 822; minuet in g BWVanh 116; musette in d BWVanh 126; polonaise in g minor BWVanh 119; polonaise in e from french suite BWV 817; polonaise in g minor BWVanh 123; prelude in c from wohltemperiertes klavier BWV 846; two-part inventions in f minor BWV 780; two-part inventions in f BWV 779; two-part inventions in a minor BWV 784; two-part inventions in b flat BWV 785

recorded for the educo piano record label and listed in 1953 american schwann catalogues
lp: educo 3001
cd: doremi DHR 7929-7930

BELA BARTOK (1881-1945)

evening in the country, from ten easy pieces sz 39

recorded in the vanguard studios new york city
lp: vanguard VSD 71249
cd: vanguard OVC 8087/08 910071

fifteen hungarian peasant songs sz 71

recorded for the educo piano label and listed in 1953 american schwann catalogues
lp: educo 3008

recorded in the vanguard studios new york city
lp: vanguard VSD 71249
cd: vanguard OVC 8087/08 910071

ballade, from fifteen hungarian peasant songs sz 39

televised by radio canada montreal on 31 january 1961
dvd: video artists international 4359

for children sz 42, volume one

recorded for the educo piano label and listed in the 1953 american schwann catalogues
lp: educo 3008
numbers 1, 4, 6, 10, 12, 14, 15, 17 and 18 are played both in their original versions and in a 1945 revision

for children sz 42, twelve pieces from volume one

recorded in the vanguard studios new york city
lp: vanguard VSD 71249
cd: vanguard OVC 8087/08 910071
the selected pieces are numbers 1, 2, 3, 5, 6, 9, 12, 17, 18, 19, 20 and 21

bartok/**romanian folk dances sz 56**

recorded in abbey road studios london on 23 august 1938
78: parlophone R 20435/PXO 1026
lp: decca (usa) DL 4011
cd: pearl GEM 0055/naxos 8.111121/erato 2564 624223

televised by radio canada montreal on 25 january 1960
dvd: video artists international 4359

recorded at a concert in tokyo bunka kaikan on 14 june 1967
cd: king records KKC 2074-2075

recorded in the vanguard studios new york city
lp: vanguard VSD 71249
cd: vanguard OVC 8087/08 910071

sonatina in d sz 55

recorded for the educo piano label and listed in 1953 american schwann catalogues
lp: educo 3008

recorded in the vanguard studios new york city
lp: vanguard VSD 71249
cd: vanguard OVC 8087/08 910071

three hungarian folk songs from the csik district sz 35a

recorded in the vanguard studios new york city
lp: vanguard VSD 71249
cd: vanguard OVC 8087/08 910071

three rondos on folk tunes sz 84

recorded in abbey road studios london on 7 october 1938 and 11 january 1939
78: parlophone R 20434-20435/PXO 1025-1026
lp: decca (usa) DL 4011
cd: pearl GEM 0055/erato 2564 624223

recorded in the vanguard studios new york city
lp: vanguard VSD 71249
cd: vanguard OVC 8087/08 910071

LUDWIG VAN BEETHOVEN (1770-1827)

piano concerto no 3 in c minor op 37

recorded in brahmssaal of the vienna musikverein between 4-6 october 1951
wiener symphoniker/rudolf moralt
lp: vox PL 7270

recorded in hilversum and published in 1962
amsterdam philharmonic society/gianfranco rivoli
lp: concert hall M 2236/M 2285/musical masterpiece society MMS 2236
cd: scribendum SC 018

piano concerto no 4 in g op 58

recorded in vienna konzerthaus and published in 1961
orchester der wiener staatsoper/victor desarzens
lp: concert hall M 2192/M 2294/musical masterpiece society MMS 2192/
vanguard SRV 252/prestige de la musique SR 9613/monitor MCS 2092
cd: scribendum SC 018/ages 509 0042

fantasy for piano, chorus and orchestra op 80

recorded in hilversum and published in 1962
chorus & orchestra of the amsterdam philharmonic society/gianfranco rivoli
lp: concert hall M 2236/musical masterpiece society MMS 2236
cd: scribendum SC 018

rondo in b flat for piano and orchestra Wo06

recorded in vienna konzerthaus and published in 1961
orchester der wiener staatsoper/victor desarzens
lp: concert hall M 2192/musical masterpiece society MMS 2192/
vanguard SRV 252/prestige de la musique SR 9613
cd: ages 509 0042

piano sonata no 8 in c minor op 13 "pathetique"

recorded for the educo piano label and listed in 1953 american schwann catalogues
lp: educo 3006

recorded in vienna in 1960
lp: concert hall M 2221/M 6236/musical masterpiece society
MMS 2221/festival classique FC 403

beethoven/**piano sonata no 17 in d minor op 31 no 2 "tempest"**

recorded in salle adyar paris in january 1954
lp: ducretet-thomson 320C 017
cd: erato 2564 624223

piano sonata no 19 in g minor op 49 no 1

recorded for the educo piano label and listed in 1953 american schwann catalogues
lp: educo 3006

recorded in vienna in 1960
lp: concert hall M 2221/M 6239/musical masterpiece society MMS 2221/festival classique FC 403
cd: ages 509 0042

piano sonata no 20 in g op 49 no 2

recorded for the educo piano label and listed in 1953 american schwann catalogues
lp: educo 3006

piano sonata no 21 in c op 53 "waldstein"

recorded in sale adyar paris in january 1955
lp: ducretet-thomson 320C 008/DTL 93108
cd: emi 562 8312/erato 2564 624223

recorded in vienna in 1960
lp: concert hall M 2221/M 6240/musical masterpiece society MMS 2221/festival classique FC 403
cd: ages 509 0042

piano sonata no 30 in e flat op 109

recorded in salle adyar paris in 1955
lp: ducretet-thomson 320C 008/DTL 93108
cd: emi 562 8312/erato 2564 624223

variations and fugue in e flat op 35 "eroica"

recorded in abbey road studios london on 27 july and 28 august 1939
78: parlophone R 20470-20472/SW 8078-8080
cd: pearl GEM 0055/toshiba YMCD 1063

recorded in salle adyar paris in 1953
lp: ducretet-thomson 32C 017
cd: erato 2564 624223

beethoven/**bagatelles op 119: nos 1, 2, 3, 4, 9, 10 and 11; minuet no 2 in g Wo0 10; albumblatt in a minor Wo0 49 "für elise"**
recorded for the educo piano label and listed in 1953 american schwann catalogues
lp: educo 3006

violin sonata in d op 12 no 1
recorded in brahmssaal of vienna musikverein in january 1955
with willi boskovsky (violin)
lp: discophiles francais DF 167
cd: erato 2564 624223

violin sonata in a op 12 no 2
recorded in abbey road studios london on 30 november 1936
with szymon goldberg (violin)
78: odeon 0 8385-8386/decca (usa) 29033-29034
cd: music and arts CD 1225/dante LYS 444-445/erato 2564 624223

recorded in brahmssaal of vienna musikverein in january 1955
with willi boskovsky (violin)
lp: discophiles francais DF 167
cd: erato 2564 624223

violin sonata in e flat op 12 no 3
recorded in brahmssaal of vienna musikvrerein in january 1955
with willi boskovsky (violin)
lp: discophiles francais DF 167
cd: erato 2564 624223

violin sonata in a minor op 23
recorded in brahmssaal of vienna musikverein in january 1955
with willi boskovsky (violin)
lp: discophiles francais DF 168
cd: erato 2564 624223

beethoven/**violin sonata in f op 24 "spring"**

recorded in the columbia studios tokyo in april 1936
with szymon goldberg (violin)
78: columbia (japan) JB 531-533/odeon 0 123838-123841/
decca (usa) 29026-29028
cd: music and arts CD 665/CD 1225/opus kura OPK 2055/
dante LYS 444-445/erato 2564 624223

recorded in brahmssaal of vienna musikverein in january 1955
with willi boskovsky (violin)
lp: discophiles francais DF 168
cd: erato 2564 624223

violin sonata in a op 30 no 1

recorded in the columbia studios tokyo in april 1936
with szymon goldberg (violin)
78: columbia (japan) JB 655-657/odeon 0 177253-177255/
decca (usa) 29035-29037
cd: music and arts CD 1225/erato 2564 624223

recorded in paris salle adyar in may 1955
with willi boskovsky (violin)
lp: discophiles francais DF 169
cd:erato 2564 624223

violin sonata in c minor op 30 no 2

recorded in paris sale adyar in may 1955
with willi boskovsky (violin)
lp: discophiles francais DF 170
cd: erato 2564 624223

violin sonata in g op 30 no 3

recorded in brahmssaal of vienna musikverein in january 1955
with willi boskovsky (violin)
lp: discophiles francais DF 168
cd: erato 2564 624223

bbc recording in the maida vale studios london on 9 june 1966
with norbert brainin (violin)
lp: bbc records and tapes REF 313
cd: bbc legends BBCL 22313

beethoven/**violin sonata in a op 47 "kreutzer"**
recorded in abbey road studios london between 4-7 december 1936 and on 27 april 1937
with szymon goldberg (violin)
78: parlophone R 20478-20481/SW 8085-8088/
odeon 0 123828-123831/decca (usa) 29029-29032
cd: music and arts CD 665/CD 1225/dante LYS 444-445/
opus kura OPK 2055/andante 1090/erato 2564 624223

recorded in paris sale adyar in may 1955
with willi boskovsky (violin)
lp: discophiles francais DF 169
cd: erato 2564 624223

violin sonata in g op 96
recorded in abbey road studios london on 23 april 1937
with szymon goldberg (violin)
78: parlophone R 20383-20385/odeon 0 123825-123827/
columbia (japan) JW 31-33
cd: music and arts CD 665/CD 1225/dante LYS 444-445/erato 2564 624223

recorded in paris salle adyar in may 1955
with willi boskovsky (violin)
lp: discophiles francais DF 170
cd: erato 2564 624223

JOHANNES BRAHMS (1833-1897)

capriccio in b op 76 no 2; intermezzi in d op 116 no 4 and in e flat and b flat op 117 nos 1 and 2; rhapsodies in g op 79 no 2 and in e flat op 119 no 4
recorded in salle adyar paris on 25-26 march 1957
lp: ducretet-thomson 300C 041
cd: emi 562 8312/erato 2564 624223

variations on a theme by schumann op 9
recorded in salle adyar paris on 25-26 march 1957
lp: ducretet-thomson 300C 041
cd: emi 562 8312/erato 2564 624223

FRIDERYK CHOPIN (1810-1849)

impromptu in f sharp op 36; prelude in e minor op 28 no 4

recorded in abbey road studios london on 30 april 1937
78: parlophone R 20451
cd: pearl GEM 0055/erato 2564 624223

valse in e minor op posth

recorded in early 1930s and listed in 1934 odeon catalogues
78: parlophone B 49613/odeon 0 11880
cd: erato 2564 624223

FRANZ JOSEF HAYDN (1732-1809)

piano sonata in d hobXVI: G1

recorded for the educo piano label
lp: educo 3005

piano sonata no 30 in d hobXVI: 19

recorded for the educo piano label
lp: educo 3005

piano sonata no 31 in a flat hobXVI: 46

recorded in paris salle adyar in march 1956
lp: discophiles francais DF 194/emi 2C051 73088
cd: erato 2564 624223

piano sonata no 32 in g minor hobXVI: 44

recorded in paris salle adyar in march 1956
lp: discophiles francais DF 194/emi 2C051 73088
cd: erato 2564 624223

piano sonata no 48 in c hobXVI: 35

recorded for the educo piano label and listed in 1953 american schwann catalogues
lp: educo 3005/3014
cd: forgotten records FR 529

piano sonata no 50 in d hobXVI: 37

recorded in the salle chopin paris in 1950
lp: vox PL 1740
cd: vox CDX2 5516

haydn/**piano sonata no 53 in e minor hobXVI: 34**

recorded in the salle adyar paris in 1953
lp: ducretet-thomson 270C 012/EL 93021
cd: emi 562 8312/forgotten records FR 184/erato 2564 624223

piano sonata no 59 in e flat hobXVI: 49

recorded in the salle adyar paris in 1953
lp: ducretet-thomson 270C 012/EL 93021
cd: emi 562 8312/forgotten records FR 184/erato 2564 624223

recorded from a radio broadcast in 1959
lp: vogue CD 672012

piano sonata no 62 in e flat hobXVI: 52

recorded in the salle chopin paris in 1950
lp: vox PL 1740

recorded in mozartsaal of the vienna konzerthaus in 1955
lp: discophiles francais DF 194/emi 2C051 73088
cd: emi 562 8312/erato 2564 624223

recorded at a concert in tokyo on 27 january 1963
cd: king records KKC 2073

andante and variations in f minor hobXVII: 6

recorded in abbey road studios london between 21-28 april 1937
78: parlophone R 20347-20348/PXO 1022-1023/
odeon 0 7820-7821
lp: decca (usa) DX 104
cd: pearl GEM 0055/erato 2564 624223

fantasy in c hobXVII: 4

recorded in the vanguard studios new york city
lp: vanguard VA 25003
cd: vanguard VBD 25003

haydn/**andante grazioso and allegro from string quartet in f, arrangement; arietta in a; minuet in c**

recorded for the educo piano label and listed in 1953 american schwann catalogues
lp: educo 3005/3014
cd: forgotten records FR 529

piano trio in f sharp minor hobXV: 26

recorded in abbey road studios london on 29 august 1939
with szymon goldberg (violin) and anthony pini (cello)
78: parlophone SW 21-22/odeon 0 177272-177273
lp: decca (usa) DL 8507/DX 104
cd: dante LYS 450/toshiba TOCE 7651-7653/
music and arts CD 1225/erato 2564 624223

piano trio in c hobXV: 27

recorded in abbey road studios london on 29 august 1939
with szymon goldberg (violin) and anthony pini (cello)
78: parlophone SW 23-24/odeon 0 177274-177275
lp: decca (usa) DL 8507/DX 104
cd: dante LYS 450/toshiba TOCE 7651-7653/
music and arts CD 1225/erato 2564 624223

piano trio in e flat hobXV: 29

recorded in abbey road studios london on 1 september 1939
with szymon goldberg (violin) and anthony pini (cello)
78: parlophone SW 25-26/odeon 0 177270-177271
lp: decca (usa) DL 8508/DX 104
cd: dante LYS 450/toshiba TOCE 7651-7653/
music and arts CD 1225/erato 2564 624223

WOLFGANG AMADEUS MOZART (1756-1791)

piano concerti arranged from works by raupach, honauer, schobert, eckard and c.p.e. bach : in f K37, in b flat K39, in d K40 and in g K41

recorded in new york city in 1966-1967
vienna festival orchestra/stephen simon
lp: epic BSC 161/SC 6061/columbia (usa) P12 11806

piano concerto in d K175

recorded in new york city in 1966-1967
vienna festival orchestra/stephen simon
lp: epic BSC 161/SC 6061/columbia (usa) P12 11806

piano concerto in b flat K238

recorded in new york city in 1966-1967
vienna festival orchestra/stephen simon
lp: epic BSC 161/SC 6061/columbia (usa) P12 11806

piano concerto in c K246 "lützow"

recorded in new york city in 1966-1967
vienna festival orchestra/stephen simon
lp: epic BSC 161/SC 6061/columbia (usa) P12 11806

mozart/**piano concerto in e flat K271 "jeunehomme"**

recorded in abbey road studios london on 25 may and 2 june 1948
philharmonia orchestra/walter susskind
78: parlophone R 20570-20573/SW 8104-8107
cd: dutton CDBP 9811/forgotten records FR/erato 2564 624223
forgotten records edition incorrectly dated 1939

recorded in mozartsaal of the vienna konzerthaus in november 1955
kammerorchester des wiener konzerthauses/willi boskovsky
lp: discophiles francais DF 176/DF 730 045
cd: doremi DHR 7929-7930/forgotten records FR 815 /
erato 2564 624223

recorded in vienna konzerthaus in february 1959
orchester der wiener staatsoper/victor desarzens
lp: concert hall M 2191/M 2912/musical masterpiece
society MMS 2191/festival classique FC 423/
monitor MCS 2105
cd: preludio PHC 1131/denon COCO 6605/
scribendum SC 018

recorded in new york city in 1966-1967
vienna festival orchestra/stephen simon
lp: epic BSC 156/SC 6056 /columbia (usa) P12 11806

piano concerto in e flat K271, third movement

televised in the national education television and radio center new york on 10 november 1967
mozart chamber orchestra/stephen simon
unpublished video recording

piano concerto in f K413

recorded in new york city in 1966-1967
vienna festival orchestra/stephen simon
lp: epic BSC 156/SC 6056/columbia (usa) P12 11806

mozart/**piano concerto in a K414**

recorded in symphony hall boston on 12 april 1953
boston symphony orchestra/pierre monteux
lp: victor LM 1783/victor (italy) A12R 0100
cd: victor (japan) BVCC 37345/urania SP 4228

recorded in new york city in 1966-1967
vienna festival orchestra/stephen simon
lp: epic BSC 154/SC 6054/columbia (usa) P12 11806

piano concerto in c K415

recorded in new york city in 1966-1967
vienna festival orchestra/stephen simon
lp: epic BSC 162/SC 6062/columbia (usa) P12 11806

piano concerto in e flat K449

recorded in new york city in 1966-1967
vienna festival orchestra/stephen simon
lp: epic BSC 162/SC 6062/columbia (usa) P12 11806

piano concerto in b flat K450

recorded in new york city in 1966-1967
vienna festival orchestra/stephen simon
lp: epic BSC 162/SC 6062/columbia (usa) P12 11806

piano concerto in d K451

recorded in new york city in 1966-1967
vienna festival orchestra/stephen simon
lp: epic BSC 162/SC 6062/columbia (usa) P12 11806

mozart/**piano concerto in g K453**

recorded in new york city in 1966-1967
vienna festival orchestra/stephen simon
lp: epic BSC 156/SC 6056/columbia (usa) P12 11806

televised in the national education television and radio center new york on 10 november 1967
mozart chamber orchestra/stephen simon
unpublished video recording

piano concerto in b flat K456

recorded in abbey road studios london on 25 march and 13 april 1938
london philharmonic orchestra/walter goehr
78: parlophone R 20404-20407/SW 8035-8038/
columbia (japan) JW 572-575
lp: decca (usa) DL 8505
cd: dutton CDBP 9811/erato 2564 624223

recorded in symphony hall boston on 13 april 1953
boston symphony orchestra/pierre monteux
lp: victor LM 1783/victor (italy) A12R 0100
cd: victor (japan) BVCC 37345/urania SP 4228

recorded in new york city in 1966-1967
vienna festival orchestra/stephen simon
lp: epic BSC 154/SC 6054/columbia (usa) P12 11806

mozart/**piano concerto in f K459**

recorded in brahmssaal of the vienna musikverein in september 1951
wiener symphoniker/rudolf moralt
lp: vox PL 6890
cd: vox CDX2 5510
world's encyclopedia of recorded music named conductor as jean-baptiste mari

recorded in hilversum in december 1960
amsterdam philharmonic society/gianfranco rivoli
lp: concert hall M 2243/musical masterpiece society MMS 2243/monitor MCS 2089
cd: scribendum SC 018/fnac 642 310

recorded in new york city in 1966-1967
vienna festival orchestra/stephen simon
lp: epic BSC 156/SC 6056/columbia (usa) P12 11806

piano concerto in d minor K466

recorded in salle pleyel paris on 2-3 march 1950
paris pro musica orchestra/enrique jorda
78: polydor (france) A 6350-6353
lp: vox PL 6290
cd: vox CDX2 5510

recorded in mozartsaal of the vienna konzerthaus in november 1954
kammerorchester des wiener konzerthauses/willi boskovsky
lp: discophiles francais DF 176
cd: doremi DHR 7929-7930/forgotten records FR 815/erato 2564 624223

recorded in new york city in may 1965
vienna festival orchestra/stephen simon
lp: epic BSC 154/SC 6054/columbia (usa) P12 11806

televised in the national education television and radio center new york on 10 november 1967
mozart chamber orchestra/stephen simon
unpublished video recording

mozart/**piano concerto in c K467**

recorded in new york city in 1966-1967
vienna festival orchestra/stephen simon
lp: epic BSC 162/SC 6062/columbia (usa) P12 11806

piano concerto in e flat K482

recorded in brahmssaal of the vienna musikverein between 19 september-6 october 1951
wiener symphoniker/rudolf moralt
lp: vox PL 7290/VBX 110
cd: vox CDX2 5516

recorded in new york city in 1966-1967
vienna festival orchestra/stephen simon
lp: epic BSC 156/SC 6056/columbia (usa) P12 11806

piano concerto in a K488

recorded in brahmssaal of the vienna musikverein on 19 september 1951
wiener symphoniker/rudolf moralt
lp: vox PL 6890
cd: vox CDX2 5510

recorded in new york city in 1966-1967
vienna festival orchestra/stephen simon
lp: epic BSC 154/SC 6054/columbia (usa) P12 11806

piano concerto in c minor K491

recorded in brahmssaal of the vienna musikverein in september 1951
wiener symphoniker/rudolf moralt
lp: vox PL 6880
cd: vox CDX2 5510
world's encyclopedia of recorded music named conductor as jean-baptiste mari

recorded in new york city in 1966-1967
vienna festival orchestra/stephen simon
lp: epic BSC 154/SC 6054/columbia (usa) P12 11806

mozart/**piano concerto in c K503**

recorded in new york city in 1966-1967
vienna festival orchestra/stephen simon
lp: epic BSC 161/SC 6061/columbia (usa) P12 11806

piano concerto in d K537 "coronation"

recorded in brahmssaal of the vienna musikverein between 19 september-15 october 1951
wiener symphoniker/rudolf moralt
lp: vox PL 7300
cd: vox CDX2 5516

recorded in hilversum in december 1960
amsterdam philharmonic society/gianfranco rivoli
lp: concert hall M 2243/M 2726/M 2944/musical masterpiece society MMS 2243/festival classique FC 455/ monitor MCS 2089
cd: scribendum SC 018/preludio PHC 1131/fnac 642 310

recorded in new york city in 1966-1967
vienna festival orchestra/stephen simon
lp: epic BSC 154/SC 6054/columbia (usa) P12 11806

piano concerto in b flat K595

recorded in new york city in 1966-1967
vienna festival orchestra/stephen simon
lp: epic BSC 162/SC 6062/columbia (usa) P12 11806

rondo in d for piano and orchestra K382

recorded in brahmssaal of the vienna musikvereins between 12-14 october 1951
wiener symphoniker/rudolf moralt
lp: vox PL 7290
cd: vox CDX2 5510

mozart/**piano sonata in c K279**

recorded in paris salle adyar in february-march 1954
lp: haydn society HSL 121-127/discophiles francais DF 97/
emi 2C051 30133
cd: music and arts CD 1001/erato 2564 624223

recorded in columbia studios new york city between 25-27 march 1968
lp: columbia (usa) Y3-33220
cd: sony SM4K 47222/82876 888082

piano sonata in f K280

recorded in paris salle adyar in february-march 1954
lp: haydn society HSL 121-127/discophiles francais DF 97/
emi 2C051 30133
cd: music and arts CD 1001/erato 2564 624223

recorded in columbia studios new york city between 4-6 march 1968
lp: columbia (usa) Y3-33220
cd: sony SM4K 47222/82876 888082

piano sonata in b flat K281

recorded in paris salle adyar in february-march 1954
lp: haydn society HS 9013/HSL 121-127/
discophiles francais DF 96 /emi 2C051 30132
cd: music and arts CD 1001/erato 2564 624223

recorded in columbia studios new york city between 27-30 october 1967
lp: epic BC 1382/columbia (usa) Y3-33320
cd: sony SM4K 47222/82876 888082/88691 928222

piano sonata in e flat K282

recorded in paris salle adyar in february-march 1954
lp: haydn society HS 9014/HSL 121-127/
discophiles francais DF 91/emi 2C051 30127
cd: music and arts CD 1001/toshiba TOCE 6721-6724

recorded in columbia studios new york city on 30 october 1967
and 6 march 1968
lp: epic BC 1385/Columbia (usa) Y3-33220
cd: sony SM4K 47222/82876 888082

mozart/**piano sonata in g K283**

recorded in paris salle adyar in february-march 1954
lp: haydn society HS 9013/HSL 121-127/
discophiles francais DF 91/emi 2C051 30127
cd: music and arts CD 1001/erato 2564 624223

recorded in columbia studios new york city between 27-30 october 1967
lp: epic BC 1382/columbia (usa) Y3-33220
cd: sony SM4K 47222/82876 888082

piano sonata in d K284 "dürnitz"

recorded in paris salle adyar in february-march 1954
lp: haydn society HS 9056/HSL 121-127/emi 2C051 30128
cd: music and arts CD 1001/erato 2564 624223

recorded in columbia studios new york city between 4-6 march 1968
lp: columbia (usa) Y3-33220
cd: sony SM4K 47222/82876 888082

piano sonata in c K309

recorded in paris salle adyar in february-march 1954
lp: haydn society HSL 121-127/discophiles francais DF 95/
emi 2C051 30131
cd: music and arts CD 1001/toshiba TOCE 6721-6724

recorded in columbia studios new york city between 3-6 may 1968
lp: columbia (usa) Y3-33220
cd: sony SM4K 47222/82876 888082

mozart/**piano sonata in a minor K310**

recorded in the salle chopin paris between 1-6 march 1950
lp: vox PL 6310/classic (france) CLC 6027
cd: vox CDX2 5516

recorded in paris salle adyar in february-march 1954
lp: haydn society HSL 121-127/discophiles francais DF 95/ emi 2C051 30131
cd: music and arts CD 1001/erato 2564 624223

recorded in the columbia studios new york city between 25-27 march 1968
lp: epic BC 1385/columbia (usa) Y3-33220
cd: sony SM4K 47222/82876 888082

piano sonata in d K311

recorded in paris salle adyar in february-march 1954
lp: haydn society HS 9013/HSL 121-127/discophiles francais DF 96/emi 2C051 30132
cd: music and arts CD 1001/erato 2564 624223

recorded in the columbia studios new york city between 4-6 march 1968
lp: columbia (usa) Y3-33220
cd: sony SM4K 47222/82876 888082

piano sonata in c K330

recorded in paris salle adyar in february-march 1954
lp: haydn society HS 9013/HSL 127-131/discophiles francais DF 91/emi 2C051 30127
cd: music and arts CD 1001/erato 2564 624223

recorded in the columbia studios new york city on 25 march 1968
lp: epic BC 1385/columbia (usa) Y3-33220
cd: sony SM4K 47222/82876 888082/ 88691 928222

mozart/**piano sonata in a K331**

recorded in the salle chopin paris between 28 february-6 march 1950
lp: vox PL 6310/classic (france) CLC 6027
cd: vox CDX2 5510

recorded in paris salle adyar in february-march 1954
lp: haydn society HS 9013/HSL 121-127/discophiles francais DF 96/emi 2C051 30132
cd: music and arts CD 1001/erato 2564 624223

recorded in vienna konzerthaus in february 1959
lp: concert hall M 2191/M 534/M 2912/musical masterpiece society MMS 2191/monitor MCS 2105/ festival classique FC 423

televised by radio montreal canada on 31 january 1961
dvd: video artists international 4359

recorded in the columbia studios new york city between 3-6 may 1968
lp: columbia (usa) Y3-33224
cd: sony SM4K 47222/82876 888082/88691 928222

rondo alla turca, from sonata in a K331

recorded in early 1930s and listed in 1934 odeon catalogues
78: parlophone B 49613/odeon 0 11880
cd: erato 2564 624223

recorded at a concert in tokyo bunka kaikan on 14 june 1967
cd: king records KKC 2074-2075

mozart/**piano sonata in f K332**

recorded in the salle chopin paris on 7-8 february 1951
lp: vox PL 7040
cd: vox CDX2 5510

recorded in paris salle adyar in february-march 1954
lp: haydn society HS 9044/HSL 121-127/discophiles francais DF 93/emi 2C051 30129
cd: music and arts CD 1001/erato 2564 624223

recorded from a radio broadcast in 1961
lp: vogue CD 672 012

recorded in the columbia studios new york city between 25-27 march 1968
lp: columbia (usa) Y3-33224
cd: SM4K 47222/82876 888082

piano sonata in b flat K333

recorded in abbey road studios london on 7 may and 8 november 1948
78: parlophone R 20566-20567
cd: erato 2564 624223

recorded in paris salle adyar in february-march 1954
lp: haydn society HS 9037/HSL 121-127/discophiles francais DF 92/emi 2C051 30128
cd: music and arts CD 1001/erato 2564 624223

recorded in the columbia studios new york city between 3-6 may 1968
lp: columbia (usa) Y3-33224
cd: sony SM4K 47222/82876 888082/88691 928222

mozart/**piano sonata in c minor K457**

recorded in abbey road studios london on 28 february and 12 april 1939
78: parlophone R 20439-20441/SW 8058-8060/PXO 1027-1030
cd: erato 2564 624223

recorded in paris salle adyar in february-march 1954
lp: haydn society HS 9056/HSL 121-127/discophiles francais DF 94/emi 2C051 30130
cd: music and arts CD 1001/erato 2564 624223

recorded in the salle adyar paris in march 1954
lp: ducretet-thomson 270C 012/concert hall M 181/ musical masterpiece society MMS 181
cd: forgotten records FR 184

recorded at a concert in tokyo on 27 january 1963
cd: king records KKC 2073

recorded in columbia studios new york city between 27-30 october 1967
lp: epic BC 1382/columbia (usa) Y3-33224
cd: sony SM4K 47222/82876 888082

piano sonata in c K545 "sonata facile"

recorded in brahmssaal of the vienna musikverein in september 1951
lp: vox PL 6880

recorded for the educo piano label and listed in 1953 american schwann catalogues
lp: educo 3014
cd: forgotten records FR 529

recorded in paris salle adyar in february-march 1954
lp: haydn society HS 9037/HSL 121-127
cd: music and arts CD 1001/erato 2564 624223

recorded in the columbia studios new york city between 25-27 march 1968
lp: columbia (usa) Y3-33224
cd: sony SM4K 47222/82876 888082

mozart/**piano sonata in b flat K570**

recorded in paris salle adyar in february-march 1954
lp: haydn society HSL 121-127/discophiles francais DF 97/ emi 2C051 30135
cd: music and arts CD 1001/erato 2564 624223

recorded in the columbia studios new york city between 4-6 march 1968
lp: Columbia (usa) Y3-33224
cd: sony SMK4 47222/82876 888082

piano sonata in d K576

recorded in the salle chopin paris on 7-8 february 1951
lp: vox PL 7040
cd: vox CDX2 5516

recorded in paris salle adyar in february-march 1954
lp: haydn society HS 9044/HSL 121-127/discophiles francais DF 93/emi 2C051 30129
cd: music and arts CD 1001/erato 2564 624223

recorded in the columbia studios new york city between 25-27 march and on 16 may 1968
lp: columbia (usa) Y3-33224
cd: sony SM4K 47222/82876 888082

piano sonata in d for 4 hands K381

recorded for the educo piano label
lp: educo 3002
kraus plays both parts for this recording

adagio in c K356; allegro in b flat K3; minuet in f K2

recorded for the educo piano label and listed in 1953 american schwann catalogues
lp: educo 3014
cd: forgotten records FR 529

mozart/**adagio in b minor K540**

recorded in abbey road studios london on 24 august 1938
78: parlophone R 20445
cd: erato 2564 624223

recorded in brahmssaal of the vienna musikverein on 15 october 1951
lp: vox PL 7300
cd: vox CDX2 5516

recorded in paris salle adyar in february-march 1954
lp: discophiles francais DF 95/emi 2C051 30131
cd: music and arts CD 1001/erato 2564 624223

recorded in vienna in 1959
45: concert hall M 947/musical masterpiece society MMS 947
lp: festival classique FC 455

allegro in g minor K312

recorded for the educo piano label and listed in 1953 american schwann catalogues
lp: educo 3014
cd: forgotten records FR 529

recorded in paris salle adyar in february-march 1954
lp: haydn society HS 9013/HSL 121-127/discophiles francais DF 92/emi 2C051 30128
cd: music and arts CD 1001/erato 2564 624223

fantasy in c K396

recorded in paris salle adyar in february-march 1954
lp: haydn society HS 9044/HSL 121-127/discophiles francais DF 93/emi 2C051 30129
cd: music and arts CD 1001/erato 2564 624223

mozart/**fantasy in d minor K397**

recorded for the educo piano label and listed in 1953 american schwann catalogues
lp: educo 3014
cd: forgotten records FR 529

recorded in paris salle adyar in february-march 1954
lp: haydn society HS 9013/HSL 121-127/discophiles francais DF 96/emi 2C051 30132
cd: music and arts CD 1001/erato 2564 624223

televised by radio canada montreal on 25 january 1960
dvd: video artists international 4359

recorded in the vanguard studios new york city
lp: vanguard VA 25003
cd: vanguard VBD 25003

recorded in the columbia studios new york city between 25-27 march 1968
lp: columbia (usa) 3216 0380/Y3-33224
cd: sony SM4K 47222/82876 888082

fantasy in c minor K475

recorded in the abbey road studios london on 12 april 1939
78: parlophone R 20438-20439/SW 8058-8061/ PXO 10327-1030
cd: erato 2564 624223

recorded in paris salle adyar in february-march 1954
lp: haydn society HS 9056/HSL 121-127/discophiles francais DF 94/emi 2C051 30130
cd: music and arts CD 1001/erato 2564 624223

recorded at a concert in tokyo on 27 january 1963
cd: king records KKC 2073

recorded in the columbia studios new york city between 27-30 october 1967
lp: columbia (usa) 3216 0380
cd: sony SM4K 47222/82876 888082

mozart/**minuet in d K355**

recorded in the salle chopin paris on 6 march 1950
78: polydor (france) A 6353
lp: vox PL 6290
cd: vox CDX2 5510

recorded in paris salle adyar in february-march 1954
lp: haydn society HSL 121-127/discophiles francais DF 95/
emi 2C051 30131
cd: music and arts CD 1001/erato 2564 624223

rondo in d K485

recorded in abbey road studios london on 26 november 1937
78: parlophone R 20397-20398
cd: erato 2564 624223

recorded in the salle chopin paris on 6 march 1950
lp: vox PL 6290

recorded in vienna in 1959
45: concert hall M 947/musical masterpiece society MMS 947
lp: festival classique FC 455

recorded in the columbia studios new york city between
25-27 march 1968
lp: columbia (usa) 3216 0380/Y3-33224
cd: sony SM4K 47222/82876 888082

rondo in a K511

recorded in brahmssaal of the vienna musikverein in september 1951
lp: vox PL 6890

recorded in paris salle adyar in february-march 1954
lp: haydn society HSL 121-127/discophiles francais DF 97/
emi 2C051 30133
cd: music and arts CD 1001/erato 2564 624223

mozart/**variations on la belle francoise K353**

recorded in paris salle adyar in february-march 1954

lp: haydn society HS 9037/HSL 121-127/discophiles francais DF 92/emi 2C051 30128

cd: music and arts CD 1001/erato 2564 624223

variations on salve tu domine K398

recorded in paris salle adyar in february-march 1954

lp: haydn society HSL 121-127/discophiles francais DF 91/ emi 2C051 30127

cd: music and arts CD 1001/erato 2564 624223

variations on unser dummer pöbel meint K455

recorded in the abbey road studios london on 26 november 1937

78: parlophone R 20397-20398

cd: erato 2564 624223

televised by radio canada montreal on 25 january 1960

dvd: video artists international 4359

recorded from a radio broadcast in 1961

lp: vogue CD 672 012

recorded at a concert in tokyo on 27 january 1963

cd: king records KKC 2073

variations on come un agnello K460

recorded in paris salle adyar in february-march 1954

lp: haydn society HS 9044/HSL 121-127/discophiles francais DF 93/emi 2C051 30129

cd: music and arts CD 1001/erato 2564 624223

eine kleine gigue K574

recorded in paris salle adyar in february-march 1954

lp: haydn society HSL 121-127/discophiles francais DF 95/ emi 2C051 30131

cd: music and arts CD 1001/erato 2564 624223

mozart/**6 early violin sonatas attributed to mozart K55-60**

recorded in vienna musikvereinssaal between june 1954-december 1955
with willi boskovsky (violin)
lp: discophiles francais/emi 2C151 73111-73118
cd: emi 763 8372/erato 2564 624223
also issued on lp by alpha and haydn society

violin sonata in c K6; violin sonata in g K27

recorded in paris salle adyar on 16 december 1955
with willi boskovsky (violin)
lp: discophiles francais DF 188/alpha DB 77/
emi 2C151 73111-73114
cd: emi 763 8372/erato 2564 624223

violin sonata in c K296

recorded in the abbey road studios london on 5 november 1935
with szymon goldberg (violin)
78: parlophone SW 7-13/SW 8007-8013/P 18/
odeon 0 8759-8760
lp: decca (usa) DL 8500/DX 103
cd: pearl GEMMCD 9454/toshiba TOCE 6175-6179/dante LYS 402/
music and arts CD 665/CD 1225/erato 2564 624223

recorded in vienna musikvereinssaal in june 1954
with willi boskovsky (violin)
lp: discophiles francais DF 123/alpha DB 72/
haydn society HSLP 133/emi 2C151 73111-73114
cd: emi 763 8372/erato 2564 624223

mozart/**violin sonatas in g K301, in e flat K302, in c K303, in e minor K304 and in a K305**

recorded in vienna musikvereinssaal in june 1954
with willi boskovsky (violin)
lp: discophiles francais DF 121-122/emi 2C151 73111-73114
cd: emi 763 8372/erato 2564 624223
also issued on lp by alpha and haydn society

violin sonata in f K376

recorded in paris salle adyar between 16-27 december 1955
with willi boskovsky (violin)
lp: discophiles francais DF 186/alpha DB 75/
emi 2C151 73115-73118
cd: emi 763 8372/erato 2564 624223

recorded in the bbc maida vale studios london on 13 april 1965
with norbert brainin (violin)
lp: bbc records and tapes REF 313
cd: bbc legends BBCL 22313

violin sonata in f K377

recorded in paris salle adyar between 16-27 december 1955
with willi boskovsky (violin)
lp: discophiles francais DF 186/alpha DB 75/
emi 2C151 73115-73118/erato 2564 624223
cd: emi 763 8372

violin sonata in b flat K378

recorded in the abbey road studios london between 16-20 april 1937
with szymon goldberg (violin)
78: parlophone SW 14-20/P 19
lp: decca (usa) DL 8502/DX 103
cd: pearl GEMMCD 9454/toshiba TOCE 6175-6179/
dante LYS 402/music and arts CD 665/CD 1225/
erato 2564 624223

recorded in vienna musikvereinssaal in june 1954
with willi boskovsky (violin)
lp: discophiles francais DF 123/haydn society HSLP 133/
alpha DB 72/emi 2C151 73115-73118
cd: emi 763 8372/erato 2564 624223

mozart/**violin sonata in g K379**

recorded in the abbey road studios london on 25 may and 6 november 1935
with szymon goldberg (violin)
78: parlophone SW 7-13/SW 8007-8013/P 18/
odeon 0 8761-8762/columbia (japan) W 118-119
lp: decca (usa) DL 8502/DX 103
cd: pearl GEMMCD 9454/toshiba TOCE 6175-6179/
music and arts CD 665/CD 1225/erato 2564 624223

recorded in vienna musikvereinssaal in june 1954
with willi boskovsky (violin)
lp: discophiles francais DF 124/alpha DB 73/
emi 2C151 73115-73118
cd: emi 763 8372/erato 2564 624223

violin sonata in e flat K380

recorded in the abbey road studios london on 20-21 april 1937
with szymon goldberg (violin)
78: parlophone SW 14-20/P 19
lp: decca (usa) DL 8501/DX 103
cd: pearl GEMMCD 9454/toshiba TOCE 6175-6179/
music and arts CD 665/CD 1225/dante LYS 402/erato 2564 624223

recorded in paris salle adyar on 19-20 december 1955
with willi boskovsky (violin)
lp: discophiles francais DF 187/alpha DB 76/
emi 2C151 73115-73118
cd: emi 763 8372/erato 2564 624223

violin sonatas in a K402 and in c K403

recorded in paris salle adyar between december 1955-may 1957
with willi boskovsky (violin)
lp: discophiles francais /emi 2C151 73115-73118
cd: emi 763 8372/erato 2564 624223
also issued on lp by alpha

mozart/**violin sonata in c K404**

recorded in abbey road studios london on 21 april 1937
with szymon goldberg (violin)
78: parlophone R 20407/SW 8035/P 25
lp: decca (usa) DL 8505/DX 103
cd: toshiba TOCE 6175-6179/dante LYS 410/music and arts CD 665/CD 1225/dutton CDBP 9811/erato 2564 624223

recorded in paris salle adyar on 2 may 1957
with willi boskovsky (violin)
lp: discophiles francais DF 187/alpha DB 76/emi 2C151 73115-73118
cd: emi 763 8372/erato 2564 624223

violin sonata in b flat K454

recorded in vienna musikvereinssaal in june 1954
with willi boskovsky (violin)
lp: discophiles francais DF 122/haydn society HSLP 132/alpha DB 71/emi 2C151 73115-73118
cd: emi 763 8372/erato 2564 624223

violin sonata in b flat K454, arrangement for flute and piano

recorded for the educo piano label in 1954
with jean-pierre rampal (flute)
lp: educo 3076
cd: horizons 070 142

violin sonata in e flat K481

recorded in the abbey road studios london on 25 may 1936
with szymon goldberg (violin)
78: parlophone SW 7-13/SW 8007-8013/P 19/odeon 0 124010-124012/0 8282-8283
lp: decca DL 8500/DX 103
cd: pearl GEMMCD 9454/toshiba TOCE 6175-6179/dante LYS 402/music and arts CD 665/CD 1225/erato 2564 624223

recorded in vienna musikvereinssaal in june 1954
with willi boskovsky (violin)
lp: discophiles francais DF 124/haydn society HSLP 134/alpha DB 73/emi 2C151 73115-73118
cd: emi 763 8372/erato 2564 624223

mozart/**violin sonatas in a K526 and in f K547**

recorded in paris salle adyar between 16-27 december 1955
with willi boskovsky (violin)
lp: discophiles francais/emi 2C151 73115-73118
cd: emi 763 8372/erato 2564 624223
also issued on lp by alpha

oboe concerto fragment K293b, arranged for violin and piano

bbc recording 1973
with norbert brainin (violin)
unpublished radio broadcast

piano trio in b flat (divertimento) K254

recorded in vienna musikvereinssaal in october 1954
with willi boskovsky (violin) and nikolaus hübner (cello)
lp: haydn society HS 9001/discophiles francais DF 81/DF 97/emi 2C151 73052-73054
cd: emi 769 7962/Toshiba TOCE 6731-6733/ andromeda ANDRCD 5149/erato 2564 624223

three piano trio movements K442

recorded in vienna musikvereinssaal in october 1954
with willi boskovsky (violin) and nikolaus hübner (cello)
lp: discophiles francais DF 82/haydn society HS 9003/ emi 2C151 73052-73054
cd: emi 769 7962/toshiba TOCE 6731-6733/ andromeda ANDRCD 5149/erato 2564 624223

piano trio in g K496

recorded in vienna musikvereinssaal in october 1954
with willi boskovsky (violin) and nikolaus hübner (cello)
lp: haydn society HS 9001/discophiles francais DF 81/DF 97/emi 2C151 73052-73054
cd: emi 769 7962/toshiba TOCE 6731-6733/ andromeda ANDRCD 5149/erato 2564 624223

mozart/**piano trio in e flat K498 "kegelstatt"**

recorded in paris salle adyar in 1955
with pierre pasquier (viola) and francois etienne (clarinet)
lp: discophiles francais DF 164
cd: doremi DHR 7929-7930/erato 2564 624223

piano trios in b flat K502 and in e K542

recorded in vienna musikvereinssaal in october 1954
with willi boskovsky (violin) and nikolaus hübner (cello)
lp: haydn society HS 9002/discophiles francais
DF 82/DF 98/emi 2C151 73052-73054
cd: emi 769 7962/toshiba TOCE 6731-6733/
andromeda ANDRCD 5149/erato 2564 624223

piano trios in c K548 and in g K564

recorded in vienna musikvereinssaal in october 1954
with willi boskovsky (violin) and nikolaus hübner (cello)
lp: haydn society HS 9003/discophiles francais
DF 83/DF 99/emi 2C151 73052-73054
cd: emi 769 7962/toshiba TOCE 6731-6733/
andromeda ANDRCD 5149/erato 2564 624223

piano quintet in e flat K452

recorded in 1956
with pierre perlot (oboe), jacques lancelot (clarinet),
paul hongne (bassoon) and gilbert coursier (horn)
lp: discophiles francais DF 164
cd: doremi DHR 7929-7930/horizons 070 142/erato 2564 624223

adagio and rondo K617

recorded in paris sale adyar in 1955
with jean-pierre rampal (flute), pierre perlot (oboe),
paul hongne (bassoon), pierre pasquier (viola) and
etienne pasquier (cello)
lp: discophiles francais DF 164
cd: doremi DHR 7929-7930/horizons 070 142/erato 2564 624223
kraus plays glass harmonica in this performance

FRANZ SCHUBERT (1797-1828)

piano sonata in a D664

recorded in the vanguard studios new york city in 1979
lp: vanguard VCS 10074
cd: vanguard OVC 8200/VAN 9098/08 406971

piano sonata in a minor D784

recorded in the abbey road studios london on 23 november 1937
78: parlophone R 20388-20390/AR 1100-1102/
SW 8032-8034/odeon 0 7854-7855
lp: decca (usa) DL 8506
cd: toshiba SGR 8213/erato 2564 624223

recorded from a radio broadcast in 1959
lp: vogue CD 672 012

piano sonata in a minor D845

recorded in abbey road studios london on 5-6 may and 4 june 1948
78: parlophone R 20585-20588/SW 8111-8114
lp: decca (usa) DL 8518
cd: erato 2564 624223

recorded in the vanguard studios new york city in 1979
lp: vanguard VCS 10074
cd: vanguard OVC 8200/VAN 8098/08 406971

piano sonata in a D959

recorded in the salle chopin paris on 6-7 february 1951
lp: vox PL 6940

recorded in Vienna in march 1959
lp: concert hall M 2178/musical masterpiece society
MMS 2178/festival classique FC 458
cd: fnac 642 328

recorded at a concert in tokyo bunka kaikan on 14 june 1967
cd: king records KKC 2074-2075

piano sonata in b flat D960

recorded in the vanguard studios new york city in 1979
lp: vanguard VSD 71267
cd: vanguard OVC 8200/VAN 8099/08 407071

schubert/**fantasy in c D760 "wanderer"**

recorded in the vanguard studios new York city in 1979

lp: vanguard

cd: vanguard OVC 8200/VAN 8099/
VBD 25003/08 407071

fantasy in c D760 "wanderer", arranged by liszt for piano and orchestra

radio concert in san francisco on 4 march 1951

san francisco symphony orchestra/pierre monteux

cd: music and arts CD 1192

orchestra described on this recording as standard symphony orchestra

fantasy in c D605a "grazer"

televised by radio canada montreal

dvd: video artists international 4359

this claimed to be the first performance of a rediscovered work

recorded in the columbia studios new york city

lp: columbia (usa) 3216 0380

grazer galop D925

recorded at a concert in tokyo bunka kaikan on 14 june 1967

cd: king records KKC 2074-2075

deutsche tänze D974

recorded in the columbia studios new york city

lp: columbia (usa) 3216 0380

divertissement a l'hongroise for 4 hands D818

recorded in the salle adyar paris on 16-17 april 1956

with homero de magalhaes (piano)

lp: discophiles francais/disques alpha DB 66

cd: emi 586 4712/erato 2564 624223

ecossaises from D145 and D783

recorded in Vienna in march 1959

lp: concert hall M 2178/musical masterpiece society
MMS 2178/festival classique FC 458

cd: fnac 642 328

schubert/**impromptu in c minor D899 no 1**

recorded for the educo piano label
lp: educo 3007

recorded in Vienna in march 1959
45: concert hall M 947/musical masterpiece society MMS 947
cd: fnac 642 328

recorded in the vanguard studios new york city in 1967
lp: vanguard VCS 10031
cd: vanguard OVC 4068/OVC 8200

recorded at a concert in tokyo bunka kaikan on 14 june 1967
cd: king records KKC 2074-2075

impromptu in e flat D899 no 2

recorded in the abbey road studios london
78: parlophone R 20562
lp: decca (usa) DL 8506
cd: erato 2564 624223

televised by radio canada montreal on 25 january 1960
dvd: video artists international 4359

recorded in the vanguard studios new york city in 1967
lp: vanguard VCS 10031
cd: vanguard OVC 4068/OVC 8200

recorded at a concert in tokyo bunka kaikan on 14 june 1967
cd: king records KKC 2074-2075

impromptu in g flat D899 no 3

recorded for the educo piano label
lp: educo 3007

recorded in the vanguard studios new york city in 1967
lp: vanguard VCS 10031
cd: vanguard OVC 4068/OVC 8200

recorded at a concert in tokyo bunka kaikan on 14 june 1967
cd: king records KKC 2074-2075

schubert/**impromptu in a flat D899 no 4**

recorded in the vanguard studios new york city in 1967
lp: vanguard VCS 10031
cd: vanguard OVC 4068/OVC 8200

recorded at a concert in tokyo bunka kaikan on 14 june 1967
cd: king records KKC 2074-2075

impromptu in f minor D935 no 1

recorded in the vanguard studios new york city in 1967
lp: vanguard VCS 10031
cd: vanguard OVC 4068/OVC 8200

impromptu in a flat D935 no 2

recorded for the educo piano label
lp: educo 3007

recorded in the vanguard studios new york city in 1967
lp: vanguard VCS 10031
cd: vanguard OVC 4068/OVC 8200

impromptu in b flat D935 no 3

recorded in the abbey road studios london on 5 may and 21 september 1948
78: parlophone R 20561-20562
lp: decca (usa) DL 8506
cd: erato 2564 624223

recorded in the vanguard studios new york city in 1967
lp: vanguard VCS 10031
cd: vanguard OVC 4068/OVC 8200

impromptu in f minor D935 no 4

recorded in the vanguard studios new york city in 1967
lp: vanguard VCS 10031
cd: vanguard OVC 4068/OVC 8200

schubert/**ten landler from D145**

recorded in the abbey road studios london on 26 november 1937
78: parlophone R 20390/SW 8032/odeon 0 7855
cd: pearl GEM 0065/toshiba SGR 8213/erato 2564 624223

recorded for the educo piano label
lp: educo 3007

landler from D366

recorded in the columbia studios new york city
lp: columbia (usa) 3216 0380

ländler from D790

recorded in vienna in march 1959
lp: concert hall M 2178/musical masterpiece society MMS 2178/festival classique FC 458
cd: fnac 642 328

moment musical in c D780 no 1

recorded for the educo piano label
lp: educo 3007

recorded at a concert in tokyo bunka kaikan on 14 june 1967
cd: king records KKC 2074-2075

moment musical in a flat D780 no 2

recorded for the educo piano label
lp: educo 3007

recorded in vienna in march 1959
45: concert hall M 517/M 946
lp: concert hall M 2178/M 2726/M 6413/musical masterpiece society MMS 2178/festival classique FC 458
cd: fnac 642 328

recorded at a concert in tokyo bunka kaikan on 14 june 1967
cd: king records KKC 2074-2075

schubert/**moment musical in f minor D780 no 3**

recorded for the educo piano label
lp: educo 3007

recorded in vienna in march 1959
45: concert hall M 517
lp: concert hall M 2178/M 2726/M 6413/musical masterpiece society MMS 2178/festival classique FC 458
cd: fnac 642 328

recorded at a concert in tokyo bunka kaikan on 14 june 1967
cd: king records KKC 2074-2075

polonaises for 4 hands D824 nos 1, 3 and 4

recorded in the salle adyar paris in april 1956
with homero de magalhaes (piano)
lp: discophiles francais/disques alpha DB 66
cd: emi 586 4712/erato 2564 624223

twelve valses nobles D969

recorded in the abbey road studios london on 23 august 1938
78: parlophone R 20429
cd: pearl GEM 0065/erato 2564 624223

recorded at a concert in tokyo bunka kaikan on 14 june 1967
cd: king records KKC 2074-2075

valses sentimentales D779

recorded in vienna in march 1959
45: concert hall M 517
lp: concert hall M 2178/M 5313-5314/musical masterpiece society MMS 2178/festival classique FC 458
cd: fnac 642 328

schubert/**variations in b flat for 4 hands D603**

recorded in the salle adyar paris on 16-17 april 1956
with homero de magalhaes (piano)
lp: discophiles francais/disques alpha DB 66
cd: emi 586 4712/erato 2564 624223

violin sonatinas in d D384 and in a minor D385

recorded in the salle adyar paris between 2-6 may 1957
with willi boskovsky (violin)
lp: discophiles francais DF 215
cd: emi 586 4712/erato 2564 624223

violin sonatina in g minor D408

recorded in the salle adyar paris between 2-6 may 1957
with willi boskovsky (violin)
lp: discophiles francais DF 215
cd: emi 586 4712/erato 2564 624223

bbc recording in the memorial hall farringdon street london on 11 november 1967
with norbert brainin (violin)
lp: bbc records and tapes REF 313
cd: bbc legends BBCL 22313

violin sonatina in g minor D408, arrangement for flute and piano

recorded for the educo piano label
with jean-pierre rampal (flute)
lp: educo 3076
cd: horizons 070 142

schubert/**winterreise D911, complete song cycle**
recorded in 1950
with dodo conrad (bass)
lp: vox PL 6090
cd: forgotten records FR 592

lieder recital: grenzen der menschheit D716; der wanderer D493; die sterne D939; fischerweise D881; sei mir gegrüsst D741; der tod und das mädchen D531; an schwager kronos D369; gruppe aus dem tartarus D583; der jüngling auf dem hügel D702; der einsame D800; du liebst mich nicht D756; l'incanto degli occhi D902 no 1; il modo di prender moglie D902 no 3
recorded in vienna konzerthaus between 23 january-20 february 1955
with dodo conrad (bass)
lp:
cd: dante LYS 251

ROBERT SCHUMANN (1810-1856)

piano concerto in a minor op 54
recorded in vienna konzerthaus
orchester der wiener staatsoper/victor desarzens
lp: concert hall M 2190/M 2327/M 3077/M 6005/M 6107/M 6206/musical masterpiece society MMS 2190/festival classique FC 428/vanguard SRV 293
cd: scribendum SC 018

CARL MARIA VON WEBER (1778-1826)

konzertstück for piano and orchestra

recorded at a concert in the concertgebouw amsterdam on 17 october 1939
concertgebouworkest/pierre monteux
cd: audiophile APL 101 560/royal concertgebouw orchestra RCO 97017/guild GHCD 2349

recorded in vienna konzerthaus
orchester der wiener staatsoper/victor desarzens
45: concert hall M 198
lp: concert hall M 2327/festival classique FC 428/ vanguard SRV 293
cd: scribendum SC 018

LILI KRAUS TEACHES A MASTERCLASS

held at the mtac golde convention in long beach california
works by bach, mozart, mendelssohn, brahms, debussy and kabalevsky are played by pupils
lp: educo 5010-5011

LILI: A DOCUDRAMA BY KEN HARRISON

filmed in 1984 by fort worth productions for pbs television
unpublished video recording from the gwendolyn p. tandy film library

LILI KRAUS INTERVIEWED BY EUGENIA ZUCKERMAN

recorded for cbs television on 23 august 1986
unpublished video recording

JOHANN SEBASTIAN BACH (1685-1750)

das wohltemperierte klavier book I: 24 preludes and fugues BWV 846-869

recorded in villingen mps tonstudios in april 1972
lp: mps 13022-13024/philips 412 7941
cd: philips 412 7942/446 5422

das wohltemperierte klavier book II: 24 preludes and fugues BWV 870-893

recorded in villingen mps tonstudios in may 1973
lp: mps 13040-13043/philips 412 7941
cd: philips 412 7942/446 5482

individual versions of preludes and fugues from das wohltemperierte clavier

book I: no 1 in c BWV 846

televised in munich amerikahaus on 27 february 1981
vhs video: left 2003
laserdisc: left 2003

book I: no 1 in c BWV 846 and no 17 in a flat BWV 862; book II: no 9 in e BWV 878 and no 20 in a minor BWV 889

recorded in vienna between december 1977-january 1978
lp: amadeo AVRS 6487/AVRS 6490
cd: amadeo 472 8322

book I: no 3 in c sharp BWV 848

recorded in vienna between 13-15 november 1961
lp: amadeo AVRS 6274/149 032

book I: no 15 in g BWV 860

recorded in london west hampstead studios between 19-24 october 1947
78: decca K 28115
cd: membran 232 849

bach/**book II: no 8 in e flat minor BWV 877**

recorded in london west hampstead studios between 10-14 february 1953

lp: decca LXT 2826/LK 40216

book II: no 17 in a flat BWV 886 and no 20 in a minor BWV 889

televised in munich amerikahaus on 27 february 1981

vhs video: left 2003

laserdisc: left 2003

english suite no 2 in a minor BWV 807

recorded in london west hampstead studios between 10-14 february 1953

lp: decca LXT 2826/LK 40216

radio recording in berlin haus des rundfunks on 30 october 1966

cd: deutsche grammophon 477 8020

sarabande from english suite no 2

recorded in vienna between 1977-1978

lp: amadeo AVRS 6487

english suite no 3 in g minor BWV 808

radio recording in berlin haus des rundfunks on 27 october 1969

cd: deutsche grammophon 477 8020

televised at a concert in bonn beethovenhalle in september 1970

dvd: euroarts 205 8698

two minuets from partita no 1 in b flat BWV 825

recorded in the studios of radio geneva on 13 february 1947

78: decca K1615

cd: membran 232 849

italian concerto in f BWV 971

recorded in vienna in january 1965

lp: amadeo AVRS 206/AVRS 6342/149 033

cd: amadeo 476 3007

radio recording in berlin studio lankwitz on 10 november 1970

cd: deutsche grammophon 477 8020

bach/**chromatic fantasy and fugue BWV 903**

televised at a concert in brahmssaal of the vienna musikverein on 24 june 1964
cd: andante 2100
dvd: andante 2100

recorded in vienna between december 1977-january 1978
lp: amadeo AVRS 6487

capriccio on the departure of a beloved brother BWV 992

private recording at a concert in uppsala on 5 april 1959
cd: deutsche grammophon 477 8020

recorded at a concert in schwetzingen schlosstheater on 3 june 1959
cd: hänssler classics 93704

toccata in c minor BWV 911

private recording at a concert in trieste on 14 march 1955
cd: deutsche grammophon 477 8020/membran 232 849
membran describes this as a 1947 recording

toccata in d minor BWV 913

recorded in london west hampstead studios between 19-24 october 1947
decca unpublished

sonata for flute and basso continuo BWV 1055

recorded in vienna between december 1977-january 1978
with ernst knava (viola da gamba)
lp: amadeo AVRS 6487/AVRS 6490
cd: amadeo 472 8322
gulda plays flute and clavichord on this recording

LUDWIG VAN BEETHOVEN (1770-1827)

piano concerto no 1 in c op 15

recorded in vienna musikvereinssaal on 22 may 1951
wiener philharmoniker/karl böhm
lp: decca LXT 2627/ACL 84/ND 370/
london (usa) LLP 421
cd: philips 456 8202/decca 467 1542/475 6835/
membran 232 849/233 021

recorded at a concert in vienna konzerthaus on 21 january 1953
wiener symphoniker
cd: orfeo C745 071B
gulda directs from the keyboard on this recording

recorded at a concert in berlin hochschule für musik on 10-11 february1957
rias-orchester/paul hindemith
lp: cetra concerto live LO 527

recorded at a concert in tokyo on 22 february 1967
nhk symphony orchestra/wolfgang sawallisch
cd: king records KKC 2005

recorded in vienna sofiensäle in june 1970 and april 1971
wiener philharmoniker/horst stein
lp: decca SDDE 304-307/SKB 25060/
london (usa) STS 15203-15206
cd: decca 461 4072/466 4272

beethoven/**piano concerto no 2 in b flat op 19**

recorded in vienna baumgarten casino on 19 october 1960
orchester der wiener staatsoper/paul angerer
lp: amadeo AVRS 6211/vanguard VRS 1080/
VSD 2106/philips A04307L/838 207AY
orchestra described on this recording as gulda-sinfonieorchester

recorded in vienna sofiensäle in june 1970 and april 1971
wiener philharmoniker/horst stein
lp: decca SDDE 304-307/SKB 25060/
london (usa) STS 15203-15206
cd: decca 450 1022/461 4072/466 4272/467 4242

piano concerto no 3 in c minor op 37

recorded at a concert in cologne funkhaus on 25 february 1957
sinfonieorchester des westdeutschen rundfunks/mario rossi
cd: medici MM 0242/membran 232 750/232 849

recorded in vienna sofiensäle in june 1970 and april 1971
wiener philharmoniker/horst stein
lp: decca SDDE 304-307/SKB 25060/
london (usa) STS 15203-15206
cd: decca 450 1022/461 4072/466 4272/467 4242

beethoven/**piano concerto no 4 in g op 58**

recorded at a concert in vienna konzerthaus on 21 january 1953
wiener symphoniker
cd: orfeo C745 071B/archipel ARPCD 0277
gulda directs from the keyboard on this recording

recorded at a concert in lugano kursaal on 14 may 1965
orchestra della radiotelevisione svizzera italiana/
andre cluytens
cd: aura AUR 163/ermitage ERM 155

recorded at a concert in tokyo on 2 may 1969
nhk symphony orchestra/lovro von matacic
cd: king records KKC 2005

recorded in vienna sofiensäle in june 1970 and april 1971
wiener philharmoniker/horst stein
lp: decca SDDE 304-307/SKB 25060/
london (usa) STS 15203-15206
cd: decca 450 0222/461 4072/466 4272/467 4242

recorded at a concert in hamburg musikhalle in may 1993
sinfonieorchester des norddeutschen rundfunks
cd: ndr klassik-extra 258 406
gulda directs from the keyboard on this recording

beethoven/**piano concerto no 5 in e flat op 73 "emperor"**

recorded in vienna konzerthaus in 1963
orchester der wiener staatsoper/hans swarowsky
lp: concert hall M 2307/M 6001-6013/M 6201-6212/
musical masterpiece society MMS 2307
cd: scribendum SC 016/ages 509 0072

televised at a concert in vienna musikvereinssaal on 5 june 1966
wiener philharmoniker/george szell
cd: andante 2100
dvd: andante 2100

recorded in vienna sofiensäle in june 1970 and april 1971
wiener philharmoniker/horst stein
lp: decca SDDE 304-307/SKB 25060/
london (usa) STS 15203-15206
cd: decca 450 0222/461 4072/466 4272

televised at a concert in munich philharmonie im gasteig on 20 july 1989
münchner philharmoniker
laserdisc: pioneer PLMBC 00651
dvd: pioneer PC 10474
gulda directs from the keyboard on this recording

piano sonatas no 1 in f minor op 2 no 1 and no 3 in c op 2 no 3

recorded in vienna ravag funkhaus on 8-9 october 1953
cd: orfeo C808 109B

recorded in london west hampstead studios on 15-16 february 1954
lp: decca LXT 2938/KD 11004 (no 1)
cd: decca 475 6835

recorded in klagenfurt orf studios in 1967
lp: amadeo AVRS 1101/AVRS 6434 (no 1)/
AVRS 6435 (no 3)/89 007/ricordi AOCL 116 000
cd: philips 415 1932/435 9122/brilliant 92773

beethoven/**piano sonata no 2 in a op 2 no 2**

recorded in vienna ravage funkhaus on 8-9 october 1953
cd: orfeo C808 109B

recorded in london west hampstead studios on 15-16 february 1954
lp: decca LXT 2958/KD 11004
cd: decca 475 6835

recorded at a concert in salzburg mozarteum on 29 july 1964
cd: orfeo C591 021B

recorded in klagenfurt orf studios in 1967
lp: amadeo AVRS 1101/AVRS 6434/89 007/
ricordi AOCL 116 000
cd: philips 415 1932/435 9122/brilliant 92773

piano sonatas no 4 in e flat op 7 and no 5 in c minor op 10 no 1

recorded in vienna ravage funkhaus on 15-16 october 1953
cd: orfeo C808 109B

recorded in london carlton rooms between 27-29 september 1955
lp: decca LXT 5140/london (usa) LLP 1372
cd: decca 475 6835

recorded in klagenfurt orf studios in 1967
lp: amadeo AVRS 1101/AVRS 6435 (no 4)/
AVRS 6435 (no 5)/89 007/ricordi AOCL 116 000
cd: philips 415 1932/ 435 9122/brilliant 92773

beethoven/**piano sonatas no 6 in f op 10 no 2 and no 7 in d op 10 no 3**

recorded in vienna ravag funkhaus on 15-16 october 1953
cd: orfeo C808 109B

recorded in london carlton rooms between 27-29 september 1955
lp: decca LXT 5141/london (usa) LLP 1374
cd: decca 475 6835

recorded in klagenfurt orf studios in 1967
lp: amadeo AVRS 1101/AVRS 6436/89 007/
ricordi AOCL 116 000
cd: philips 415 1932/ 435 9122/brilliant 92773

piano sonata no 8 in c minor op 13 "pathetique"

recorded in vienna ravag funkhaus on 22 october 1953
cd: orfeo C808 109B

recorded in london conway hall between 30 september-5 october 1957
lp: london (usa) LLP 3022
cd: decca 475 6835/membran 232 849

recorded in vienna in 1960
lp: concert hall M 2364/M 2916/M 6236/
musical masterpiece society MMS 2364
cd: scribendum SC 016

recorded in klagenfurt orf studios in 1967
lp: amadeo AVRS 204/AVRS 1101/AVRS 6437/
89 007/149 035/ricordi AOCL 116 000
cd: philips 415 1932/ 431 1172/435 9122/
brilliant 92773

recorded at a concert in vienna konzerthaus on 5 september 1986
cd: amadeo 423 0222

beethoven/**piano sonata no 9 in e flat op 14 no 1**

recorded in vienna ravag funkhaus on 22 october 1953
cd: orfeo C808 109B

recorded in london conway hall between 30 september-5 october 1957
lp: london (usa) LLP 3022
cd: decca 475 6835/membran 232 849

recorded in klagenfurt orf studios in 1967
lp: amadeo AVRS 1101/AVRS 6437/89 007/
ricordi AOCL 116 000
cd: philips 415 1932/ 435 9122/brilliant 92773

piano sonata no 10 in g op 14 no 2

recorded in vienna ravag funkhaus on 22 october 1953
cd: orfeo C808 109B

recorded in london conway hall between 30 september-5 october 1957
lp: london (usa) LLP 3022
cd: decca 475 6835/membran 232 849

radio recording by rias berlin on 17 january 1959
cd: audite 21404

recorded at a concert in schwetzingen schlosstheater on 3 june 1959
cd: hänssler classics 93704

recorded in klagenfurt orf studios in 1967
lp: amadeo AVRS 1101/AVRS 6437/89 007/
ricordi AOCL 116 000
cd: philips 415 1932/ 435 9122/brilliant 92773

beethoven/**piano sonata no 11 in b flat op 22**

recorded in vienna ravag funkhaus on 26 october 1953
cd: orfeo C808 109B

recorded in london kingsway hall between 16-20 december 1957
lp: decca ECS 724
cd: decca 475 6835

recorded in klagenfurt orf studios in 1967
lp: amadeo AVRS 1101/AVRS 6438/89 007/
ricordi AOCL 116 000
cd: philips 415 1932/435 9122/brilliant 92773

piano sonatas no 12 in a flat op 26 "funeral march" and no 13 in e flat op 27 no 1

recorded in vienna ravag funkhaus on 29 october 1953
cd: orfeo C808 109B

recorded in london kingsway hall between 16-20 december 1957
lp: decca ECS 724
cd: decca 475 6835

recorded in klagenfurt orf studios in 1967
lp: amadeo AVRS 1101/AVRS 6434 (no 12)/
AVRS 6442 (no 13)/89 007/ricordi AOCL 116 000
cd: philips 415 1932/435 9122/brilliant 92773

beethoven/**piano sonata no 14 in c sharp minor op 27 no 2 "moonlight"**

recorded in london west hampstead studios in december 1949
78: decca AX 561-562
lp: decca LXT 2581/ACL 84/ND 730/
london (usa) LLP 150
cd: pearl GEM 0166

recorded in vienna ravage funkhaus on 1 november 1953
cd: orfeo C808 109B

recorded in london kingsway hall between 16-20 december 1957
lp: decca ECS 720
cd: decca 443 0122/475 6835

recorded in vienna in 1960
lp: musical masterpiece society MMS 990
cd: scribendum SC 016

recorded at a concert in salzburg mozarteum on 29 july 1964
cd: orfeo C591 021B

recorded in klagenfurt orf studios in 1967
lp: amadeo AVRS 1101/AVRS 6438/149 035/
89 007/ricordi AOCL 116 000
cd: philips 415 1932/431 1172/ 435 9122/
brilliant 92773

piano sonata no 15 in d op 28 "pastoral"

recorded in vienna ravage funkhaus on 29 october 2953
cd: orfeo C808 109B

recorded in london kingsway hall between 16-20 december 1957
lp: decca ECS 720
cd: decca 443 0122/475 6835

recorded in klagenfurt orf studios in 1967
lp: amadeo AVRS 1101/AVRS 6440/89 007/
ricordi AOCL 116 000
cd: philips 415 1932/ 435 9122/brilliant 92773

beethoven/**piano sonatas no 16 in g op 31 no 1 and no 18 in e flat op 31 no 3**

recorded in vienna ravag funkhaus on 6 november 1953
cd: orfeo C808 109B

recorded in london kingsway hall between 16-20 december 1957
lp: decca ECS 725/teldec 641 840AG
cd: decca 475 6835

recorded in klagenfurt orf studios in 1967
lp: amadeo AVRS 1101/AVRS 6439 (no 16)/
AVRS 6441 (no 18)/89 007/ricordi AOCL 116 000
cd: philips 415 1932/435 9122/brilliant 92773

piano sonata no 17 in d minor op 31 no 2 "tempest"

recorded in vienna ravage funkhaus on 6 november 1953
cd: orfeo C808 109B

recorded in london kingsway hall between 16-20 december 1957
lp: decca ECS 725/teldec 641 840AG
cd: decca 443 0122/475 6835

recorded in klagenfurt orf studios in 1967
lp: amadeo AVRS 1101/AVRS 6441/89 007/
ricordi AOCL 116 000
cd: philips 415 1932/435 9122/brilliant 92773

piano sonata no 19 in g minor op 49 no 1

recorded in vienna ravag funkhaus on 15-16 october 1953
cd: orfeo C808 109B

recorded in london west hampstead studios on 15-16 february 1954
lp: decca LXT 2938
cd: decca 475 6835

recorded in klagenfurt orf studios in 1967
lp: amadeo AVRS 1101/AVRS 6440/89 007/
ricordi AOCL 116 000
cd: philips 415 1932/435 9122/brilliant 82773

beethoven/**piano sonata no 20 in g op 49 no 2**

recorded in vienna ravag funkhaus on 15-16 october 1953
cd: orfeo C808 109B

recorded in london west hampstead studios on 15-16 february 1954
lp: decca LXT 2938
cd: decca 475 6835

recorded in vienna in 1960
lp: concert hall M 2364/M 2916/M 6240/
musical masterpiece society MMS 2364
cd: scribendum SC 016

recorded in klagenfurt orf studios in 1967
lp: amadeo AVRS 1101/AVRS 6441/89 007/
ricordi AOCL 116 000
cd: philips 415 1932/435 9122/brilliant 92773

piano sonata no 21 in c op 53 "waldstein"

recorded in vienna ravag studios on 6 november 1953
cd: orfeo C808 109B

recorded in vienna sofiensäle between 8-12 september 1958
lp: decca ECS 722/teldec 641 844AF
cd: decca 443 0122/475 6835

recorded in klagenfurt orf studios in 1967
lp: amadeo AVRS 1101/AVRS 6442/89 007/
ricordi AOCL 116 000
cd: philips 415 1932/431 1172/435 9122/
brilliant 92773

recorded in lugano by radiotelevisione svizzera italiana on 19 january 1968
cd: aura AUR 112

beethoven/**piano sonata no 22 in f op 54**

recorded in vienna ravag funkhaus on 13 november 1953
cd: orfeo C808 109B

recorded in vienna sofiensäle between 6-12 september 1958
lp: decca ECS 720
cd: decca 443 0122/475 6835/testament SBT 1301

recorded in klagenfurt orf studios in 1967
lp: amadeo AVRS 1101/AVRS 6437/89 007/
ricordi AOCL 116 000
cd: philips 415 1932/435 9122/brilliant 92773

piano sonata no 23 in f minor op 57 "appassionata"

recorded in vienna ravag funkhaus on 20 november 1953
cd: orfeo C808 109B

recorded by westdeutscher rundfunk in cologne funkhaus on 22 february 1957
cd: medici MM 0242

recorded in vienna sofiensäle between 6-12 september 1958
lp: decca ECS 721/641 844AF
cd: decca 443 0122/466 4272/475 6835

recorded in vienna in 1960
lp: concert hall M 2364/M 2916/M 6236/
musical masterpiece society MMS 2354
cd: scribendum SC 016

recorded in klagenfurt orf studios in 1967
lp: amadeo AVRS 204/AVRS 1101/AVRS 6438/
89 007/149 035/ricordi AOCL 116 000
cd: philips 415 1932/431 1172/435 9122/
brilliant 92773

beethoven/**piano sonatas no 24 in f sharp op 78 and no 25 in g op 79**

recorded in vienna ravag funkhaus between 13-27 november 1953
cd: orfeo C808 109B

recorded in vienna sofiensäle between 8-12 september 1958
lp: decca ECS 721
cd: decca 443 0122 (no 24)/466 4272 (no 24)/475 6835

recorded in klagenfurt orf studios in 1967
lp: amadeo AVRS 1101/AVRS 6441/89 007/
ricordi AOCL 116 000
cd: philips 415 1932/435 9122/brilliant 92773

piano sonata no 26 in e flat op 81a "les adieux"

recorded in geneva victoria hall in november 1950
lp: decca LXT 2594/ACL 274/KD 11004/
london (usa) LLP 312
cd: pearl GEM 0166/decca 475 6835/membran 233 021

recorded in vienna ravag funkhaus on 20 november 1953
cd: orfeo C808 109B

recorded in klagenfurt orf studios in 1967
lp: amadeo AVRS 204/AVRS 1101/AVRS 6442/
89 007/ricordi AOCL 116 000
cd: philips 415 1932/431 1172/435 9122/
brilliant 92773

beethoven/**piano sonata no 27 in e minor op 90**

recorded in vienna ravag funkhaus on 20 november 1953
cd: orfeo C808 109B

recorded in vienna sofiensäle between 8-12 september 1958
lp: decca ECS 721
cd: decca 475 6835

recorded in vienna konzerthaus in 1963
cd: scribendum SC 016/ages 509 007

recorded in klagenfurt orf studios in 1967
lp: amadeo AVRS 1101/AVRS 6439/89 007/
ricordi AOCL 116 000
cd: philips 415 1932/435 9122/brilliant 92773

piano sonata no 28 in a op 101

recorded by rias berlin in kleistsaal on 27 january 1950
cd: audite AU 21404/membran 233 031/
archipel ARPCD 0336

recorded in vienna ravag funkhaus on 11 january 1954
cd: orfeo C808 109B

recorded in cologne funkhaus by westdeutscher rundfunk on 22 february 1957
cd: medici MM 0242

recorded in vienna sofiensäle between 8-12 september 1958
lp: decca ECS 722
cd: decca 475 6835

recorded in klagenfurt orf studios in 1967
lp: amadeo AVRS 1101/AVRS 6441/89 007/
ricordi AOCL 116 000
cd: philips 415 1932/435 9122/brilliant 92773

beethoven/**piano sonata no 29 in b flat op 106 "hammerklavier"**

recorded in vienna musikvereinssaal in may 1951
lp: decca LXT 2624/london (usa) LLP 412
cd: decca 475 6835/membran 233 021

recorded in vienna ravag funkhaus on 11 january 1954
cd: orfeo C808 109B

recorded in klagenfurt orf studios in 1967
lp: amadeo AVRS 1101/AVRS 6443/89 007/
ricordi AOCL 116 000
cd: philips 415 1932/431 1172/ 435 9122/
brilliant 92773

televised at a concert in bonn beethovenhalle on 15 september 1970
dvd: euroarts 205 8698

piano sonata no 30 in e op 109

recorded in vienna ravage funkhaus on 26 november 1953
cd: orfeo C808 109B

recorded in vienna sofiensäle between 8-12 september 1958
lp: decca ECS 723
cd: decca 475 6835

recorded by rias berlin on 17 january 1959
cd: audite AU 21404

recorded in klagenfurt orf studios in 1967
lp: amadeo AVRS 11091/AVRS 6443/89 007/
ricordi AOCL 116 000
cd: philips 415 1932/435 9122/brilliant 92773

beethoven/**piano sonata no 31 in a flat op 110**

recorded in london west hampstead studios between 5-8 december 1949
78: decca AX 396-398
lp: decca LXT 2581/london (usa) LLP 150
cd: pearl GEM 0166

recorded in vienna ravag funkhaus on 26 november 1953
cd: orfeo C808 109B

recorded in vienna sofiensäle between 8-12 september 1958
lp: decca ECS 723
cd: decca 475 6835

recorded at a concert in schwetzingen schlosstheater on 3 june 1959
cd: artists' live recordings FED 058/hänssler classics 93704

recorded at a concert in vienna in 1959
cd: golden melodram GM 40066

recorded at a concert in salzburg mozarteum on 29 july 1964
cd: orfeo C591 021B

recorded in klagenfurt orf studios in 1967
lp: amadeo AVRS 1101/AVRS 6444/89 007/
ricordi AOCL 116 000
cd: philips 415 1932/435 9122/brilliant 92773

recorded in vienna between december 1977-january 1978
lp: amadeo AVRS 6490
cd: amadeo 472 8322

recorded at a concert in montpellier cour jacques coeur on 31 july 1993
cd: accord 476 1894

beethoven/**piano sonata no 32 in c minor op 111**

recorded in vienna ravag funkhaus on 27 november 1953
cd: orfeo C808 109B

recorded in vienna sofiensäle between 8-12 september 1958
lp: decca ECS 723
cd: decca 443 0122/475 6835

recorded at a concert in salzburg mozarteum on 29 july 1964
cd: orfeo C591 021B

recorded at a concert in vienna musikvereinssaal on 7 december 1966
lp: preiser SPR 3143/denon OW 7731
cd: preiser 90225

recorded in klagenfurt orf studios in 1967
lp: amadeo AVRS 1101/AVRS 6444/89 007/
ricordi AOCL 116 000
cd: philips 415 1932/435 9122/brilliant 92773

recorded in salzburg mozarteum in february1984
lp: philips 412 1141
cd: philips 412 1142

diabelli variations in c op 120

recorded in vienna orf studios in november 1957
cd: orfeo C808 109B

recorded in villingen mps tonstudios in february 1970
lp: mps 13000/eternal 827 806/ex libris 16783
cd: amadeo 429 4992/harmonia mundi HMA 190 5127

beethoven/**variations and fugue in e flat op 35 "eroica"**

recorded in geneva victoria hall in november 1950
lp: decca LXT 2594/ACL 274/KD 11004/
london (usa) LLP 312
cd: pearl GEM 0166/decca 475 6835/archipel ARPCD 0336

recorded in vienna orf studios in november 1957
cd: orfeo C808109B

recorded by rias berlin on 17 january 1959
cd: audite AU 21404

televised at a concert in bonn beethovenhalle on 15 september 1970
dvd: euroarts 205 8698

thirty variations on an original theme WoO80

recorded by rias berlin on 17 january 1959
cd: audite AU 21404

bagatelle op 119 no 2 and six bagatelles

recorded in london west hampstead studios on 5 december 1949
78: decca AX 396

bagatelles op 126 nos 2 and 3

recorded in vienna musikvereinssaal in may 1951
cd: decca 475 6835

andante favori in f WoO57; für elise in a minor WoO59; ecossaise in e WoO83

recorded in vienna between 13-15 november 1961
lp: amadeo AVRS 6274/149 032

beethoven/**violin sonata in a minor op 23**

recorded ++

with arthur grumiaux (violin)
cd: aura AUR 101

violin sonatas in c minor op 30 no 2 and in g op 96

recorded in london west hampstead studios between 24-26 february 1954

with ruggiero ricci (violin)
lp: decca LXT 2942/london (usa) LLP 1004
cd: decca 475 6835

the complete cello sonatas: in f op 5 no 1; in g minor op 5 no 2; in a op 69; in c op 102 no 1; in d op 102 no 2

recorded in brahmssaal of the vienna musikverein between 23-28 june 1959

with pierre fournier (cello)
lp: deutsche grammophon LPM 18602-18604/SLPM 138 081-138 083
cd: deutsche grammophon 437 3522/477 6266/regis RRC 2092/documents 600 096

beethoven/**variations on mozart's ein mädchen oder weibchen**

recorded in brahmssaal of the vienna musikverein between 23-28 june 1959
with pierre fournier (cello)
lp: deutsche grammophon LPM 18604/SLPM 138 083
cd: deutsche grammophon 437 3522/477 6266/
regis RRC 2092/documents 600 096

recorded in 1981
with heinrich schiff (cello)
lp: amadeo AVRS 6497/philips 6514 220

variations on mozart's bei männern welche liebe fühlen

recorded in brahmssaal of the vienna musikverein between 23-28 june 1959
with pierre fournier (cello)
lp: deutsche grammophon LPM 18603/SLPM 138 082
cd: deutsche grammophon 437 3522/477 6266/
regis RRC 2092/documents 600 096

variations on handel's see the conquering hero

recorded in brahmssaal of the vienna musikverein between 23-28 june 1959
with pierre fournier (cello)
lp: deutsche grammophon LPM 18604/SLPM 138 083
cd: deutsche grammophon 437 3522/477 6266/
regis RRC 2092/documents 600 096

piano and wind quintet in e flat op 16

recorded in vienna musikvereinssaal on 13-14 april 1960
with members of the wiener philharmoniker
lp: deutsche grammophon LPM 18638/SLPM 138 638
cd: deutsche grammophon 435 5932

GEORGES BIZET (1838-1875)

habanera from carmen, arranged by gulda

recorded at a concert in montpellier cour jacques coeur on 31 july 1993
cd: accord 476 1894

JOHANNES BRAHMS (1833-1897)

haydn variations, original version for two pianos

recorded at concerts in cologne philharmonie on 20-21 may 1988
with joe zawinul (second piano)
cd: capriccio 67175

wiegenlied, arranged by gulda

recorded at a concert in montpellier on 31 july 1993
cd: accord 476 1894

FRIDERYK CHOPIN (1810-1849)

piano concerto no 1 in e minor op 11

recorded in london kingsway hall on 18-19 february 1954
london philharmonic orchestra/adrian boult
lp: decca LXT 2925/ACL 94/LW 50096/
london (usa) LLP 1001
cd: philips 456 8202/deutsche grammophon 477 8724/
membran 233 021/documents 600 045

andante spianato and grande polonaise op 22

recorded in vienna in january 1965
lp: amadeo AVRS 6342/149 033
cd: amadeo 476 3007

chopin/**the four ballades**

recorded in london west hampstead studios on 9-10 september 1954
45: decca VD 614 (nos 1 and 3)
lp: decca LW 5156/london (usa) LD 9177
cd: philips 456 8202/membran 233 021/
archipel ARPCD 0451 (nos 1 and 4)

private recording at a concert in trieste on 24 march 1955
cd: deutsche grammophon 477 8724

ballade no 3 op 47

recorded in london west hampstead studios on 2 december 1948
78: decca K 2166
cd: membran 232 849

barcarolle in f sharp op 60

recorded by rias berlin in studio lankwitz on 17 november 1959
cd: audite AU 21404/membran 233 021

private recording at a concert in buenos aires on 5 july 1960
cd: deutsche grammophon 477 8724

televised at a concert in munich philharmonie am gasteig on 19 november 1990
cd: sony SMK 52499
laserdisc: sony SLV 46397
vhs: sony SHV 46397
dvd: arthaus 101 635

recorded at a concert in montpellier cour jacques coeur on 31 july 1993
cd: accord 476 1894

berceuse op 57; etudes op 25 nos 1 and 2

recorded in london west hampstead studios on 2-3 december 1948
78: decca K 2167
cd: membran 232 849 (berceuse and op 25 no 1)

chopin/**etude op 25 no 7**

recorded in vienna in 1962
lp: amadeo

televised at a concert in munich philharmonie am gasteig on 19 november 1990
cd: sony SMK 52499
laserdisc: sony SLV 46397
vhs: sony SHV 46397
dvd: arthaus 101 635

nocturne in f sharp op 15 no 2

private recording at a concert in buenos aires on 19 may 1956
cd: deutsche grammophon 477 8724

recorded in vienna in 1962
lp: amadeo

televised at a concert in munich philharmonie am gasteig on 19 november 1990
cd: sony SMK 52499
laserdisc: sony SLV 46397
vhs: sony SHV 46397
dvd: arthaus 101 635

recorded at a concert in montpellier cour jacques coeur on 31 july 1993
cd: accord 476 1894

chopin/**nocturne in c minor op 48 no 1**

recorded by rias berlin in studio lankwitz on 17 november 1959
cd: audite AU 21404

private recording at a concert in buenos aires on 5 july 1960
cd: deutsche grammophon 477 8724

nocturne in b op 62 no 1

recorded in vienna in 1962
lp: amadeo

private recording at a concert in munich philharmonie am gasteig on 13 july 1986
cd: deutsche grammophon 477 8724

the twenty-four preludes op 28

recorded in london west hampstead studios between 12-14 february 1953
lp: decca LXT 2837/BLK 16140/london (usa) LLP 755
prelude no 15 also on decca 45-71084

private recordings at concerts in graz and zürich between 10 march-4 april 1955
cd: deutsche grammophon 477 8724/477 8727

recorded by rias berlin in studio lankwitz on 19 november 1959
cd: audite AU 21404

the twenty-four preludes op 28: no 3 in g, no 4 in e minor, no 7 in a, no 9 in e, no 15 in d flat and no 19 in e flat

recorded at a concert in munich philharmonie im gasteig on 13 july 1986
cd: amadeo 423 0462

valse in d flat op 64 no 1

private recording at a concert in reggio emilia on 7 march 1955
cd: deutsche grammophon 477 8724

valse in e minor op posth

recorded in vienna between 13-15 november 1961
lp: amadeo AVRS 6274
cd: amadeo 476 3007

FRANCOIS COUPERIN (1668-1733)

le rossignol

recorded in 1981
lp: amadeo 427 8001
cd: amadeo 427 8002
gulda plays clavichord on this recording

CLAUDE DEBUSSY (1862-1918)

complete preludes, books 1 and 2

recorded in vienna redoutensaal between 1-3 june 1955
lp: decca LXT 5116-5117/london (usa) LLP 1289-1290
cd: philips 456 8172/membran 233 021
individual preludes from this recording also on decca 45-71097 and 45-71104

recorded in vienna orf studios in 1957
cd: andante 2110

recorded in villingen mps tonstudios in february 1969
lp: mps 52001/basf 29 28575

individual versions of preludes

les sons et les parfums/*book 1*

recorded at a concert in montpellier cour jacques coeur on 31 july 1993
cd: accord 476 1894

des pas sur la neige/*book 1*

recorded in geneva radio studios on 13 february 1947
78: decca K 1615

recorded by rias berlin on 3 march 1953
cd: audite AU 21404

debussy/individual versions of preludes/continued

ce qu'a vu le vent d'ouest; la fille aux cheveux de lin/*book 1*

recorded between 1977-1978
lp: philips 6514 226
cd: philips 415 5992

recorded at a concert in munich philharmonie am gasteig on 19 november 1990
cd: sony SMK 52499
laserdisc: sony SLV 46397
vhs: sony SHV 46397
dvd: arthaus 101 635

la serenade interrompue/*book 1*

recorded by rias berlin on 3 march 1953
cd: audite AU 21404

recorded at a concert in cour jacques coeur montpellier on 31 july 1993
cd: accord 476 1894

la puerta del vino/*book 2*

recorded at a concert in munich philharmonie am gasteig on 19 november 1990
cd: sony SMK 52499
laserdisc: SLV 46397
vhs: sony SHV 46397
dvd: arthaus 101 635

recorded at a concert in cour jacques corur montpellier on 31 july 1993
cd: accord 476 1894

ondine/*book 2*

recorded at a concert in vienna musikvereinssaal on 7 march 1966
lp: preiser SPR 3143
cd: preiser 90225

feux d'artifice/*book 2*

recorded in vienna between 13-15 november 1961
lp: amadeo AVRS 6274/AVRS 6488/149 032
cd: philips 415 5992

debussy/**pour le piano**

recorded in vienna orf studios in 1957
cd: andante 2110

recorded in london conway hall between 30 september-5 october 1957
lp: decca LXT 5415
cd: philips 456 8172/membran 233 021

recorded by rias berlin in studio lankwitz on 7 november 1959
cd: audite AU 21404

l'isle joyeuse

recorded in london west hampstead studios on 3 december 1948
78: decca M 639
cd: membran 232 849

recorded in vienna orf studios in 1957
cd: andante 2110

recorded in london conway hall in october 1957
lp: decca LXT 5415
cd: philips 456 8172/membran 233 021

reflects dans l'eau (images book 1)

recorded in london west hampstead studios on 21 october 1947
78: decca AK 1992
cd: membran 232 849

recorded in vienna orf studios in 1957
cd: andante 2110

recorded in london conway hall in october 1957
lp: decca LXT 5415
cd: philips 456 8172/membran 231 021

recorded in vienna between december 1977-january 1978
lp: amadeo AVRS 6488/AVRS 6490/philips 6514 226
cd: philips 415 5992/amadeo 472 8322

televised at a concert in munich amerikahaus on 27 february 1981
vhs video: loft 2003
laserdisc: loft 2003

debussy/**poissons d'or (images book 2)**
recorded by rias berlin on 3 march 1953
cd: audite AU 21404/membran 233 021

soiree dans grenade (estampes)
recorded by rias berlin on 3 march 1953
cd: audite AU 21404

recorded in london conway hall in october 1957
lp: decca LXT 5415
cd: philips 456 8172 /membran 233 021

televised at a concert in munich amerikahaus on 27 february 1981
vhs video: loft 2003
laserdisc: loft 2003

suite bergamasque
recorded by rias berlin in kleistsaal on 22 january 1950
cd: audite AU 21404

recorded in london west hampstead studios between 10-14 february 1953
45: decca CEP 685
lp: decca LXT 2817/LW 5278/london (usa) LLP 754
cd: philips 456 8172/membran 233 021
clair de lune from this recording also on decca 45-71084

recorded in vienna orf studios in 1957
cd: andante 2110

clair de lune (suite bergamasque)
recorded in vienna in 1961-1962
lp: amadeo

FRIEDRICH GULDA (1930-2000)

piano concerto

recorded at a concert in vienna musikvereinssaal on 29 september 1991
wiener philharmoniker
unpublished radio broadcast
gulda directs from the keyboard on this recording

selige sehnsucht

recorded at a concert in 1974
with hermann prey (baritone)/tony insolaco (percussion)
cd: philips 463 2432

GEORGE FRIDERIC HANDEL (1685-1759)

passacaglia from keyboard suite no 7 HWV432

recorded in vienna between 13-15 november 1961
lp: amadeo AVRS 6274/149 032

FRANZ JOSEF HAYDN (1732-1809)

piano sonata no 62 in e flat hobXVI:52

recorded at a concert in schwetzingen schlosstheater on 3 june 1959
lp: concert artists' recordings FED 058
cd: hänssler classics 93704

andante and variations in f minor hobXVII:6

recorded at a concert in vienna in 1959
cd: golden melodram GM 40066

recorded at a concert in schwetzingen schlosstheater on 3 june 1959
lp: concert artists' recordings FED 058
cd: hänssler classics 93704

recorded by radiotelevisione svizzera italiana in lugano on 19 january 1968
cd: aura AUR 112

WOLFGANG AMADEUS MOZART (1756-1791)

piano concerto in e flat K271 "jeunehomme"

recorded in munich herkulessaal on 30 september 1969
sinfonieorchester des bayerischen rundfunks/karl böhm
cd: golden melodram GM 40066/orfeo C263 921B
golden melodrama edition dated 2 october 1967

concerto in e flat for two pianos K365

recorded in amsterdam concertgebouw on 20 june 1983
with chick corea (second piano)
concertgebouworkest/nikolaus harnoncourt
lp: teldec 642 961AZ
cd: teldec 842 961ZK/2292 429882

piano concerto in e flat K449

recorded in london kingsway hall on 15-16 september 1954
london symphony orchestra/anthony collins
lp: decca LXT 5013/LW 5260/london (usa) LLP 1158
cd: australian eloquence 480 3442/documents 232 750

recorded at a concert in salzburg mozarteum on 2 august 1958
concertgebouworkest/wolfgang sawallisch
cd: orfeo C795 091B

recorded by südwestfunk in baden-baden on 16 january 1962
sinfonieorchester des südwestfunks/hans rosbaud
cd: passion and concentration PACO 1025

piano concerto in g K453

recorded in vienna baumgarten casino on 19 october 1960
orchester der wiener staatsoper/paul angerer
lp: amadeo AVRS 6211/149 034/vanguard VRS 1080/
VSD 2106/philips A04307L/838 207AY
cd: australian eloquence 480 3442
orchestra described on this recording as gulda-sinfonieorchester

mozart/**piano concerto in d minor K466**

recorded at a concert in vienna musikvereinssaal on 10 june 1973
wiener philharmoniker/claudio abbado
unpublished radio broadcast

recorded in vienna musikvereinssaal on 23-24 september 1974
wiener philharmoniker/claudio abbado
lp: deutsche grammophon 2530 548
cd: deutsche grammophon 415 8422/
423 6862/453 0792

recorded at a concert in vienna musikvereinssaal on 24 may 1981
wiener philharmoniker/erich leinsdorf
unpublished radio broadcast

televised at a concert in munich philharmonie am gasteig on 5 july 1986
münchner philharmoniker
dvd: pioneer 10279/arthaus 101 673
gulda directs from the keyboard on this recording

recorded at a concert in vienna musikvereinssaal on 27 september 1991
wiener philharmoniker
unpublished radio broadcast
gulda directs from the keyboard on this recording

recorded at a concert in hamburg musikhalle on 2 may 1993
sinfonieorchester des norddeutschen rundfunks
cd: emi 562 8572
gulda directs from the keyboard on this recording

piano concerto in c K467

recorded in vienna konzerthaus in june 1962
orchester der wiener staatsoper/hans swarowsky
lp: concert hall M 2319/M 6201/musical
masterpiece society MMS 2319/preiser 135 011
cd: scribendum SC 016/preiser 90021
gulda adds piano decoration during orchestral passages

recorded in vienna musikvereinssaal on 23-24 september 1974
wiener philharmoniker/claudio abbado
lp: deutsche grammophon 2530 548
cd: deutsche grammophon 415 8422/423 6862/
453 0792/477 7493

mozart/**piano concerto in a K488**

recorded at a concert in salzburg grosses festspielhaus on 4 august 1961
sächsische staatskapelle dresden/franz konwitschny
cd: orfeo C839 112B

recorded by südwestfunk in baden-baden on 15 january 1962
sinfonieorchester des südwestfunks/hans rosbaud
cd: hänssler classics 93064

recorded at a concert in munich herkulessaal in 1962
sinfonieorchester des bayerischen rundfunks/joseph keilberth
cd: golden melodram GM 40066

recorded in amsterdam concertgebouw between 21-23 september 1983
concertgebouworkest/nikolaus harnoncourt
lp: teldec 642 970AZ
cd: teldec 842 970ZK/4509 974832/85738 90912

recorded at a concert in hamburg musikhalle on 3 may 1993
sinfonieorchester des norddeutschen rundfunks
cd: emi 562 8572
gulda directs from the keyboard on this recording

piano concerto in c minor K491

recorded by rias berlin in jesus-christus-kirche between 27 february-2 march 1953
rias-sinfonieorchester/igor markevitch
cd: audite AU 21404/membran 233 021

recorded at a concert in ludwigsburg on 1 july 1959
orchester des süddeutschen rundfunks/joseph keilberth
cd: golden melodram GM 40066

mozart/**piano concerto in c K503**

recorded in london carlton rooms between 19-21 september 1955
new symphony orchestra/anthony collins
lp: decca LXT 5138/ND 369/london (usa) LLP 1370
cd: piano time (italy) PTC 2020/testament SBT 1301/
australian eloquence 480 3442/
membran 232 750/232 849

recorded at a concert in paris theatre des champs-elysees on
6 december 1956
orchestre national de l'ortf/georg solti
cd: golden melodram GM 40066

recorded in vienna musikvereinssaal between 12-26 may 1975
wiener philharmoniker/claudio abbado
lp: deutsche grammophon 2530 642
cd: deutsche grammophon 419 4792/
423 6862/453 0792

piano concerto in d K537 "coronation"

recorded in london carlton rooms between 19-21 september 1955
new symphony orchestra/anthony collins
lp: decca LXT 5138/BR 3008/LW 50080/
ND 369/london (usa) LLP 1370
cd: piano time (italy) PTC 2020/testament SBT 1301/
australian eloquence 480 3442/
membran 232 750/232 849

recorded in amsterdam concertgebouw between
21-23 september 1983
concertgebouworkest/nikolaus harnoncourt
lp: teldec 642 970AZ
cd: teldec 842 970ZK/4509 974832/85738 90912

televised at a concert in munich philharmonie am gasteig on
5 july 1986
münchner philharmoniker
dvd: pioneer 10279/arthaus 101 673
gulda directs from the keyboard on this recording

mozart/**piano concerto in d "coronation", arrangement of second movement**

televised in munich philharmonie am gasteig on 20 july 1989
cd: sony SX2K 48082
laserdisc: sony SLV 46396
vhs: sony SHV 46396

piano concerto in b flat K595

recorded in vienna konzerthaus in june 1962
orchester der wiener staatsoper/hans swarowsky
lp: concert hall M 2319/M 6201/musical masterpiece society MMS 2319/preiser 135 011
cd: scribendum SC 016/preiser 90021
gulda adds piano decoration during orchestral passages

recorded at a concert in bucharest sala de concerte on 10 september 1967
cluj philharmonic orchestra/emil simon
lp: electrocord NI 760-66

recorded at a concert in düsseldorf tonhalle on 29 november 1972
münchner philharmoniker/rudolf kempe
lp: mps 13 003/basf 29 21770/amadeo 149 034
cd: scribendum SC 004

recorded in vienna musikvereinssaal between 12-26 may 1975
wiener philharmoniker/claudio abbado
lp: deutsche grammophon 2530 642
cd: deutsche grammophon 419 4792/423 6862/
453 0792/477 7493

string divertimento K138

recorded at a concert in vienna musikvereinssaal on 27 september 1991
wiener philharmoniker
friedrich gulda conducts
unpublished radio broadcast

piano sonatas in c K279, in f K280, in b flat K281 and in g K283

private recordings in weissenbach am attersee in november 1982
cd: deutsche grammophon 477 6130/477 8466

mozart/**piano sonata in e flat K282**

televised at a concert in munich amerikahaus on 13 february 1981
vhs video: loft 2001
laserdisc: loft 2001
dvd: amadeo 60027/dream time DEBC 14821

private recording in weissenbach am attersee in november 1982
cd: deutsche grammophon 477 6130/477 8466

piano sonata in d K284 "dürnitz"

private recording in weissenbach am attersee in november 1982
cd: deutsche grammophon 477 6130/477 7152/477 8466

piano sonata in d "dürnitz", third movement

recorded at a concert in munich philharmonie am gasteig on 17 july 1988
lp: amadeo 427 8001
cd: amadeo 427 8002

piano sonata in a minor K310

recorded in london west hampstead studios between 10-14 february 1953
lp: decca LXT 2826/LK 40216
cd: australian eloquence 480 3442

recorded by radiotelevisione svizzera italiana in lugano on 19 january 1968
cd: aura AUR 112

private recording in weissenbach am attersee in november 1982
cd: deutsche grammophon 477 6130/477 7152/477 8466

mozart/**piano sonata in d K311**

private recording in weissenbach am attersee in 1980
cd: deutsche grammophon 477 6130/477 8466

televised at a concert in munich amerikahaus on 13 february 1981
vhs video: loft 2001
laserdisc: loft 2001
dvd: amadeo 60027/dream time DEBC 14821

piano sonata in c K330

recorded in 1960
lp: amadeo

private recording in weissenbach am attersee in 1980
cd: deutsche grammophon 477 6130/477 8466

piano sonata in a K331

recorded in vienna in january 1977
lp: amadeo AVRS 6481/169 061
cd: philips 431 1172

private recording in weissenbach am attersee in november 1982
cd: deutsche grammophon 477 6130/477 7152/477 8466

piano sonata in a K331, rondo alla turca

recorded in vienna between 13-15 november 1961
lp: amadeo AVRS 6274/149 032

mozart/**piano sonata in f K332**

recorded in 1960
lp: amadeo

private recording in weissenbach am attersee in 1980
cd: deutsche grammophon 477 7152/477 8466

televised at a concert in munich amerikahaus on 13 febtuary 1981
vhs video: loft 2001
laserdisc: loft 2001
dvd: amadeo 60027/dream time DEBC 14821

recorded in ibiza open mind studio in september 1998
cd: unnumbered

piano sonata in f K332, adagio only

televised at a concert in munich philharmonie am gasteig on 21 july 1989
dvd: pioneer PC 11533

televised at a concert in munich muffathalle on 23 june 1995
vhs video only

piano sonata in b flat K333

recorded in vienna in january 1977
lp: amadeo AVRS 6481/169 061
cd: philips 431 1172

private recording in weissenbach am attersee in 1980
cd: deutsche grammophon 477 7152/477 8466

televised at a concert in munich philharmonie am gasteig in 1990
dvd: pioneer 10474/arthaus 101 635

televised at a concert in munich muffathalle on 23 june 1995
dvd: pioneer PC 10474

mozart/**piano sonata in c minor K457**

televised at a concert in munich amerikahaus on 13 february 1981
vhs video: loft 2001
laserdisc: loft 2001
dvd: amadeo 60027/dream time DEBC 14821

private recording in weissenbach am attersee in november 1982
cd: deutsche grammophon 477 7152/477 8466

televised at a concert in munich philharmonie am gasteig on 20 july 1989
cd: sony SX2K 48082
laserdisc: sony SLV 46396
vhs: sony SHV 46396
dvd: arthaus 101 635/pioneer PC 11533

recorded at a concert in montpellier cour jacques coeur on 31 july 1993
cd: accord 476 1894

piano sonata in c K545 "sonata facile"

recorded in vienna in january 1965
lp: amadeo AVRS 6342/149 033

private recording in weissenbach am attersee in 1980
cd: amadeo 476 3007/deutsche grammophon 477 7152/477 8466

piano sonata in b flat K570

recorded in munich herkulessaal in september 1978
cd: deutsche grammophon 431 0842

private recording in weissenbach am attersee in november 1982
cd: deutsche grammophon 477 7152/477 8466

mozart/**piano sonata in d K576**

recorded in london west hampstead studios on 2 december 1948
78: decca AK 2168-2169
cd: australian eloquence 480 3442/membran 232 849

recorded in munich herkulessaal in september 1978
cd: deutsche grammophon 431 0842

private recording in weissenbach am attersee in november 1982
cd: deutsche grammophon 477 7152/477 8466

televised at a concert in munich muffathalle on 23 june 1995
dvd: pioneer PC 10474

recorded in linz donaupark on 13 september 1997
cd: brucknerhaus LC 4388

fantasy in d minor K397

recorded at a concert in vienna musikvereinssaal in 1978
cd: deutsche grammophon 477 8466

televised at a concert in munich philharmonie am gasteig on 21 july 1990
cd: sony SMK 52499
laserdisc: sony SLV 46397
vhs: sony SHV 46397
dvd: arthaus 101 635/pioneer PC 11533

televised at a concert in munich muffathalle on 23 june 1995
dvd: pioneer PC 10474

mozart/**fantasy in c minor K475**

recorded in munich herkulessaal in september 1978
cd: deutsche grammophon 431 0842

private recording in weissenbach am attersee in 1980
cd: deutsche grammophon 477 7152/477 8466

televised at a concert in munich amerikahaus on 13 february 1981
vhs: loft 2001
laserdisc: loft 2001
dvd: amadeo 60027/dream time DEBC 1482

televised at a concert in munich philharmonie am gasteig on 20 july 1989
cd: sony SX2K 48082
laserdisc: sony SLV 46396
vhs: sony SHV 46396
dvd: arthaus 101 635/pioneer PC 11533

recorded at a concert in montpellier cour jacques coeur on 31 july 1993
cd: accord 476 1894

rondo in d K485

recorded in london west hampstead studios between 10-14 february 1953
lp: decca LK 40216
cd: australian eloquence 480 3442

recorded in vienna between 13-15 november 1961
lp: amadeo AVRS 6274/149 032

variations on paisiello's salve tu domine K398

private recording at a concert in sao paulo in april 1956
cd: deutsche grammophon 477 8466

mozart/**piano and wind quintet in e flat K452**

recorded in vienna konzerthaus on 13-14 april 1960

with members of the wiener philharmoniker

lp: deutsche grammophon LPM 18638/SLPM 138 638

cd: deutsche grammophon 435 5932

susanna's aria from le nozze di figaro, arranged for piano by gulda

televised at a concert in munich philharmonie am gasteig on 21 july 1990

cd: sony SX2K 48082

vhs video: sony SHV 46396

laserdisc: sony SLV 46396

dvd: arthaus 101 635

recorded at a concert in montpellier cour jacques coeur on 31 july 1993

cd: accord 476 1894/deutsche grammophon 477 8466

FRANCIS POULENC (1889-1963)

les chemins de l'amour

recorded at a concert in vienna konzerthaus on 5 september 1986

jessye norman (soprano)

cd: amadeo 423 0222

SERGEI PROKOFIEV (1891-1953)

piano concerto no 3 in c op 26

recorded at a concert in hamburg musikhalle on 9 december 1957

sinfonieorchester des norddeutschen rundfunks/

hans schmidt-isserstedt

cd: green hill GH 0015-0016

piano sonata no 7 in b flat op 83

recorded in london west hampstead studios on 22 october 1947

78: decca AK 1992-1994

cd: membran 232 849

recorded by rias berlin in the kleistsaal on 27 january 1950

cd: audite AU 21404

MAURICE RAVEL (1875-1937)

gaspard de la nuit

recorded in london west hampstead studios between 10-14 february 1953
lp: decca LXT 2817/london (usa) LLP 754
cd: philips 456 8172/membran 233 021

recorded by rias berlin in the funkhaus on 3 march 1953
cd: audite AU 21404

recorded in vienna orf studios in 1957
cd: andante 2110

recorded in vienna between december 1977-january 1978
lp: amadeo AVRS 6488/AVRS 6490/philips 6514 226
cd: philips 415 5992/amadeo 472 8322

sonatine

recorded in vienna orf studios in 1957
cd: andante 2110

recorded in london conway hall between 30 september-5 october 1957
lp: decca LXT 5415
cd: philips 456 8172/membran 233 021

recorded in vienna in 1961
lp: amadeo

prelude in a minor

recorded in vienna in 1961
lp: amadeo

ravel/**toccata from le tombeau de couperin**

recorded in vienna between 13-15 november 1961

lp: amadeo AVRS 6274/149 032

cd: philips 415 5992/amadeo 476 3007

valses nobles et sentimentales

recorded in vienna orf studios in 1957

cd: andante 2110

recorded in london conway hall between 30 september-5 october 1957

lp: decca LXT 5415

cd: philips 456 8172/membran 233 021

vocalise

recorded at a concert in vienna konzerthaus on 5 september 1986

with jessye norman (soprano)

cd: amadeo 423 0222

FRANZ SCHUBERT (1797-1828)

piano sonata in a minor D845

recorded in vienna orf studios in 1967

cd: andante 2110

recorded in vienna between december 1977-january 1978

lp: amadeo AVRS 6490

cd: philips 431 1172/amadeo 423 7902/472 8322

piano sonata in b flat D960

recorded in vienna orf studios in 1967

cd: andante 2110

two scherzi D593 in b flat and d flat

recorded in vienna in january 1965

lp: amadeo AVRS 6483/149 033

cd: philips 431 1172/amadeo 423 7902/476 3007

schubert/**impromptus D899: no 1 in c minor, no 2 in e flat, no 3 in g flat and no 4 in a flat**

recorded between 1954-1956
cd: archipel ARPCD 0451

recorded at a concert in buenos aires in june 1960
lp: concert hall M 2365/musical masterpiece society MMS 2365/prestige de la musique SR 9642
cd: priceless D 14201/scribendum SC 016

recorded in vienna orf studios in 1967
cd: andante 2110

recorded by radiotelevisione svizzera italiana on 19 january 1968
cd: aura AUR 106/AUR 112

recorded in weissenbach am attersee in june 1999
cd: toshiba TOCE 91042

individual versions of impromptus D899

no 3 in g flat

televised at a concert in munich philharmonie im gasteig on 19 november 1990
cd: sony SMK 52499
laserdisc: sony SLV 46397
vhs: sony SHV 46397

recorded at a concert in montpellier cour jacques coeur on 31 july 1993
cd: accord 476 1894

no 4 in a flat

recorded in vienna between 13-15 november 1961
lp: amadeo AVRS 6274/149 032
cd: philips 431 1172/amadeo 423 7902

recorded at a concert in vienna musikvereinssaal on 7 december 1966
lp: preiser SPR 3143/denon OW 7731
cd: preiser 90225

schubert/**six moments musicaux D760**

recorded at a concert in buenos aires in june 1960
lp: concert hall M 2365/musical masterpiece society MMS 2365
cd: priceless D 14201/scribendum SC 016

recorded in vienna orf studios in 1967
cd: andante 2110

recorded in weissenbach am attersee in june 1999
cd: toshiba TOCE 91042

individual versions of moments musicaux

no 1 in b flat, no 2 in d flat and no 4 in a flat

recorded in vienna in 1961
lp: amadeo
cd: philips 431 1172

lieder: klärchens lied; gretchen am spinnrade; mignon; rastlose liebe

recorded in munich between 20-26 february 1981
with ursula anders (soprano)
lp: mps 14334
cd: paradise productions
vhs video: loft 2004
laserdisc: loft 2004

ROBERT SCHUMANN (1810-1856)

piano concerto in a minor op 54

recorded at a concert in vienna musikvereinssaal on 4 may 1955
wiener symphoniker/joseph keilberth
cd: orfeo C746 071B/hosanna HOS 06

recorded in vienna sofiensäle on 10-11 september 1956
wiener philharmoniker/volkmar andreae
lp: decca LXT 5280/ACL 136/SPA 493/MD 1008/ND 604/london (usa) LLP 1589/CM 9176/CS 6082/STS 15026
cd: decca 433 6282/pickwick PWK 1148

schumann/**fantasiestücke op 12**

recorded in london carlton rooms between 27-29 september 1955
lp: london (usa) LLP 1371
cd: australian eloquence 470 6662

recorded in salzburg mozarteum between 20-24 february 1984
lp: philips 412 1131
cd: philips 412 1132

in der nacht from fantasiestücke op 12

recorded at a concert in montpellier cour jacques coeur on 31 july 1993
cd: accord 476 1894

träumerei from kinderszenen op 15

recorded in vienna between 13-15 november 1961
lp: amadeo AVRS 6274/149 032

liederkreis op 39, song cycle

recorded in salzburg mozarteum between 20-24 february 1984
with ursula anders (soprano)
lp: philips 412 1131
cd: philips 412 1132

mondnacht

recorded in munich between 20-26 february 1981
with ursula anders (soprano)
cd: paradise productions

waldszenen op 82

recorded in london carlton rooms between 27-29 september 1955
lp: london (usa) LLP 1371

JOHANN STRAUSS II (1825-1899)

arrangements by gulda from die fledermaus: ich lade gern mir gäste ein; brüderlein schwesterlein

televised at a concert in munich philharmonie am gasteig on 19 november 1990
cd: sony SMK 52499
laserdisc: sony SLV 46397
vhs: sony SHV 46397

recorded at a concert in montpellier cour jacques coeur on 31 july 1993
cd: accord 476 1894

RICHARD STRAUSS (1864-1949)

burleske for piano and orchestra

recorded in london kingsway hall on 15-16 september 1954
london symphony orchestra/anthony collins
lp: decca LXT 5013/ND 604/ND 759/
london (usa) LLP 1158
cd: philips 456 8202/decca 460 2962/
documents 298 312/605 125

recorded at a concert in salzburg in altes festspielhaus on 25 august 1957
wiener philharmoniker/karl böhm
cd: orfeo C710 081B

der burger als edelmann, suite from the incidental music

recorded in vienna sofiensäle between 6-10 october 1966
wiener philharmoniker/lorin maazel
lp: decca LXT 6304/SXL 6304/london (usa)
CM 6537/CS 6537
cd: decca 448 3752/470 9542/australian
eloquence 480 0404

richard strauss/**lieder recital: die nacht; wie sollten wir geheim; meinem kinde; freundliche vision; säusle liebe myrthe; der stern; heimkehr; ich wollt' ein sträusslein; als dir mein lied erklang**
recorded in vienna musikvereinssaal between 6-9 september 1956
with hilde gueden (soprano)
lp: decca ECS 630/london (usa) R 23212
cd: nimbus NI 7592/membran 233 021/decca great voices

lieder recital: schlechtes wetter; schlagende herzen; befreit; einerlei
recorded in vienna musikvereinssaal between 6-9 september 1956
with hilde gueden (soprano)
45: decca CEP 593
lp: decca ECS 630/london (usa) R 23212
cd: nimbus NI 7592/membran 233 021/decca great voices

CARL MARIA VON WEBER (1778-1826)

konzertstück for piano and orchestra
recorded in vienna sofiensäle on 11 september 1956
wiener philharmoniker/volkmar andreae
45: decca CEP 567
lp: decca LXT 5280/ACL 136/MD 1008/london (usa) LLP 1158/LLP 1589/CM 9176/CS 6082/STS 15026
cd: philips 456 8202/membran 233 021/ archipel ARPCD 0336

TRADITIONAL

he's got the whole world in his hands
recorded at a concert in vienna konzerthaus on 5 september 1986
with jessye norman (soprano)
cd: amadeo 423 0222

GULDA: A SELECTION FROM THE JAZZ-INSPIRED ALBUMS

cool vienna (1955); a man of letters (1956);
friedrich gulda at birdland (1956); jazz in europe (1962);
jazz workshop concert (1962); from vienna with jazz (1964);
ineffable (1965); music for 4 soloists and band (1965);
midlife harvest (1965-1972); galgenlieder (1966);
gulda jazz (1966); gulda und sein eurojazz-orchester (1967);
golowin meets gulda (1967); jam session (1967);
the air from other planets (1969); vienna revisited (1969);
ndr jazz-werkstatt (1969); it's all one (1970);
as you like it (1970); donau so blau (1970);
the long road to freedom (1971); fata morgana (1971);
ossiach live (1971); play piano play (1971-1986);
anima (1972); chopin and beyond (1973-1986);
it's up to you (1974); gegenwart (1976);
nachricht vom lande (1976); message from gulda (1978);
tales of world music (1978); opus anders (1980);
winter meditation (1981); concerto for ursula (1982);
cello concerto (1982); epitaph for a love;
friedrich gulda and chick corea (1982); the master (1983);
piano composition (1984); landschaft mit pianist (1987);
concerto for myself (1988);
music for 2 pianos with joe zawinul (1988);
friedrich gulda and friends (1989);
mozart no end and the paradise band (1989);
gulda non-stop (1990); i love barbara (1990);
paradise island (1992); midnite party (1998);
summer dance (1998); the legacy (1998);
liberation with ursula anders
der wanderer (g'schichten aus dem golowinerwald)

certain albums also contain classical material or arrangements, which are listed in the main composer section of the discography

INGRID HAEBLER (born 1930): the discography

JOHANN SEBASTIAN BACH (1685-1750)

the six french suites BWV 812-817

recorded in amsterdam concertgebouw in 1982
lp: philips 6769 097
suite no 6 also issued on cd 456 8232

JOHANN CHRISTIAN BACH (1735-1782)

six concerti for keyboard and orchestra op 1

recorded in vienna in november 1977
capella academica wien/eduard melkus
lp: philips 6768 001
cd: philips 438 7122
haebler plays fortepiano in these recordings

six concerti for keyboard and orchestra op 7

recorded in vienna between october 1969-october 1973
capella academica wien/eduard melkus
lp: philips 6500 041 (nos 5-6)/6500 846 (nos 1-4)/
6768 001
cd: philips 438 7122
haebler plays fortepiano in these recordings

six concerti for keyboard and orchestra op 13

recorded in vienna between october 1969-october 1973
capella academica wien/eduard melkus
lp: philips 6500 041 (nos 1, 3 and 6)/6500 846 (no 4)/
6500 847 (nos 2 and 5)/6768 001
cd: philips 456 0642
haebler plays fortepiano in these recordings

johann christian bach/**six keyboard sonatas op 5**

recorded in vienna between 20-24 september 1970
lp: philips 6500 120
haebler plays fortepiano in these recordings

six keyboard sonatas op 17

recorded in vienna between 1-4 october 1973
lp: philips 6500 848
haebler plays fortepiano in these recordings

six sonatas for flute and continuo op 16

recorded in vienna between 13-17 july 1970
with kurt redel (flute)
lp: philips 6500 121
haebler plays fortepiano in these recordings

LUDWIG VAN BEETHOVEN (1770-1827)

piano concerti no 2 in b flat op 19 and no 4 in g op 58

recorded in london wembley town hall between 29-31 december 1970
new philharmonia orchestra/alceo galliera
lp: philips 6500 176/6527 028
cd: tower records (japan) PROC 1191

quintet for piano and wind op 16

recorded in salzburg mozarteum between 19-22 september 1971
with members of the bamberger symphoniker
lp: philips 6500 326

beethoven/violin sonatas in d op 12 no 1; in a op 12 no 2; in e flat op 12 no 3; in a minor op 23

recorded in la chaux de fonds between 5-14 january 1975
with henryk szeryng (violin)
lp: philips 6769 011
cd: philips 446 5212/tower records (japan) PROC 1224-1227

violin sonata in f op 24 "spring"

recorded in la chaux de fonds between 2-10 june 1978
with henryk szeryng (violin)
lp: philips 6769 011
cd: philips 420 8622/446 5212/tower records (japan) PROC 1224-1227

violin sonatas in a op 30 no 1 and in g op 30 no 3

recorded in la chaux de fonds between 2-10 june 1978
with henryk szeryng (violin)
lp: philips 6769 011
cd: philips 446 5242/tower records (japan) PROC 1224-1227

violin sonatas in c minor op 30 no 2 and in g op 96

recorded in la chaux de fonds between 11-18 august 1979
with henryk szeryng (violin)
lp: philips 6769 011
cd: philips 446 5242/tower records (japan) PROC 1224-1227

beethoven/**violin sonata in a op 47 "kreutzer"**

recorded in la chaux de fonds between 15-19 december 1979
with henryk szeryng (violin)
lp: philips 6769 011
cd: philips 420 8622/446 5242/tower records (japan) PROC 1224-1227

FRIDERYK CHOPIN (1810-1849)

complete nocturnes

recorded in vienna and published in 1961
lp: vox VUX 2007/SVUX 52007

complete valses

recorded in vienna and published in 1962
lp: vox PL 11970/GBY 11970

recorded in salzburg mozarteum in june 1970
lp: philips 6539 007
valse in e flat op 18 from this set published on cd 456 8232

FRANZ JOSEF HAYDN (1732-1809)

keyboard concerto in d hobXVIII:11

recorded in amsterdam concertgebouw between 1-3 july 1960
netherlands chamber orchestra/szymon goldberg
lp: philips 802 737LY/philips fontana 698 059CL/ 875 040CY/875 052CY/mercury MG 50414/ SR 90414
cd: philips 456 8232/473 7742/ retrospective 93407

haydn/**piano sonatas no 33 in c minor hobXVI:20 and no 34 in d hobXVI:33**

recorded in salzburg schloss klessheim between 20-28 august 1968
lp: philips 839 735LY
haebler plays fortepiano in these recordings

piano sonatas no 48 in c hobXVI:35, no 49 in c sharp minor hobXVI:36, no 50 in d hobXVI:37 and no 51 in g hobXVI:38

recorded in salzburg schloss klessheim between 20-28 august 1968
lp: philips 839 736LY
cd: philips 442 6592
haebler plays fortepiano in these recordings

piano sonata no 52 in g hobXVI:39

recorded in amsterdam concertgebouw between 1-3 july 1960
lp: philips fontana 698 026CL/CFL 1048/
philips 802 737LY/ 839 737LY/802 749LY

recorded in salzburg schloss klessheim between 20-28 august 1968
lp: philips 839 736LY
cd: philips 442 6592
haebler plays fortepiano in this recording

andante con variazioni in f minor hobXVII:6

recorded in amsterdam concertgebouw between 1-3 july 1960
lp: philips fontana 698 026CL/CFL 1048/
philips 802 737LY/839 737LY/802 749LY
cd: philips 456 8232

WOLFGANG AMADEUS MOZART (1756-1791)

piano concerti arranged from works by raupach, honauer, schobert, eckard and c.p.e. bach: in f K37, in b flat K39, in d K40 and in g K41

recorded in vienna in october 1973
capella academica wien/eduard melkus
lp: philips 6500 773/6747 375
cd: philips 454 3522/478 2695/
decca (korea) DN 0021
haebler plays fortepiano in these recordings

piano concerto in d K175

recorded in vienna konzerthaus on 7-8 may 1956
wiener symphoniker/paul walter
lp: vox PL 9830
orchestra described on this recording as vienna pro musica

recorded in london wembley town hall between 10-14 july 1965
london symphony orchestra/alceo galliera
lp: philips A02481L/835 351LY/AL 3592/SAL 3592/
AXS 12000/6717 001/6747 375
cd: philips 454 3522/decca (korea) DN 0021

piano concerto in b flat K238

recorded in vienna konzerthaus in 1955
wiener symphoniker/heinrich hollreiser
lp: vox PL 9290/eurodisc KK 71034
orchestra described on this recording as vienna pro musica

recorded in london wembley town hall on 6-7 january 1966
london symphony orchestra/witold rowicki
lp: philips 802 873LY/SAL 3728/AXS 12000/
SC75-AX 200/6717 001/6747 375
cd: philips 454 3522/decca (korea) DN 0021

mozart/**concerto for three pianos in f K242**

recorded in london wembley town hall on 5 july 1968
london symphony orchestra/alceo galliera
with ludwig hoffmann and sas bunge
(second & third pianos)
lp: philips 802 882LY/SAL 3741/AXS 12000/
SC75-AX200/6527 206/6580 144/
6717 001/6747 375
cd: philips 454 3522/decca (korea) DN 0021

piano concerto in c K246 "lützow"

recorded in vienna konzerthaus in 1955
wiener symphoniker/heinrich hollreiser
lp: vox PL 9290/eurodisc KK 71034
orchestra described on this recording as vienna pro musica

recorded in london wembley town hall on 13-14 july 1965
london symphony orchestra/alceo galliera
lp: philips A02481L/835 351LY/AL 3592/
SAL 3592/AXS 12000/6717 001/6747 375
cd: philips 454 3522/decca (korea) DN 0021

piano concerto in e flat K271 "jeunehomme"

*recorded in london wembley town hall between
9-13 january 1968*
london symphony orchestra/witold rowicki
lp: philips 802 872LY/SAL 3728/AXS 12000/
SC75-AX200/6580 083/6717 001/6747 375
cd: philips 454 3522/decca (korea) DN 0021

mozart/**concerto for two pianos in e flat K365**

recorded in london wembley town hall on 21 january 1968
london symphony orchestra/alceo galliera
with ludwig hoffmann (second piano)
lp: philips 802 882LY/SAL 3741/AXS 12000/
SC75-AX200/6527 206/6580 083/6717 001/
6747 375
cd: philips 454 3522/decca (korea) DN 0021

piano concerto in f K413

recorded in london walthamstow assembly hall on 4-5 october 1965
london symphony orchestra/colin davis
lp: philips 835 392AY/SAL 3645/BAL 30/
SBAL 30/AXS 12000/SC71-AX402/
6580 069/6717 001/6747 375
cd: philips 454 3522/decca (korea) DN 0021

piano concerto in a K414

recorded in vienna konzerthaus on 25 march 1954
wiener symphoniker/heinrich hollreiser
lp: vox PL 8710/VBX 112
orchestra described on this recording as vienna pro musica

recorded in amsterdam concertgebouw on 7 july 1960
netherlands chamber orchestra/szymon goldberg
lp: philips fontana 698 059CL/875 040CY/
875 052CY
cd: retrospective 93407

recorded in london wembley town hall between 6-11 november 1967
london symphony orchestra/witold rowicki
lp: philips 802 874LY/SAL 3753/AXS 12000/
SC75-AX200/6717 001/6747 375
cd: philips 454 3522/decca (korea) DN 0021

mozart/**piano concerto in c K415**

recorded in vienna konzerthaus on 7-8 may 1956
wiener symphoniker/paul walter
lp: vox PL 10080/VBX 112
cd: preludio PHC 3146
orchestra described on this recording as vienna pro musica

recorded in london walthamstow assembly hall on 4-5 october 1965
london symphony orchestra/colin davis
lp: philips 635 392AY/SAL 3645/BAL 30/SBAL 30/AXS 12000/C71-AX402/6717 001/6747 375
cd: philips 454 3522/decca (korea) DN 0021

piano concerto in e flat K449

recorded in london walthamstow assembly hall on 3-4 may 1965
london symphony orchestra/colin davis
lp: philips 835 364AY/SAL 3642/BAL 30/SBAL 30/AXS 12000/C71-AX402/6717 001/6747 375
cd: philips 454 3522/decca (korea) DN 0021

piano concerto in b flat K450

recorded in vienna konzerthaus in 1953
wiener symphoniker/heinrich hollreiser
lp: vox PL 8300/VBX 112
orchestra described on this recording as vienna pro musica

recorded in london walthamstow assembly hall on 19-20 september 1964
london symphony orchestra/colin davis
lp: philips A002426L/835 296LY/AL 3545/SAL 3545/BAL 30/SBAL 30/AXS 12000/C71-AX402/6570 144/6717 001/6747 375/mercury MG 50428/SR 90248
cd: philips 454 3522/478 5601/decca (korea) DN 0021

mozart/**piano concerto in d K451**

recorded in london walthamstow assembly hall on 19-20 september 1964
london symphony orchestra/colin davis
lp: philips A02426L/835 296LY/AL 3545/
SAL 3545/AXS 12000/6717 001/6747 375/
mercury MG 50428/SR 90428
cd: philips 454 3522/decca (korea) DN 0021

piano concerto in g K453

recorded in vienna konzerthaus on 23-24 february 1955
bamberger symphoniker/heinrich hollreiser
lp: vox PL 9390/VBX 111
cd: preludio PHC 3146

recorded in london wembley town hall between 4-6 june 1965
london symphony orchestra/witold rowicki
lp: philips A02438L/835 308LY/AL 3537/
SAL 3537/BAL 30/SBAL 30/AXS 12000/
C71-AX402/6580 043/6717 001/6747 375
cd: philips 454 3522/decca (korea) DN 0021

mozart/**piano concerto in b flat K456**

recorded in vienna konzerthaus in 1953
wiener symphoniker/heinrich hollreiser
lp: vox PL 8300/VBX 111
orchestra described on this recording as vienna pro musica

recorded in vienna musikvereinssaal between 9-11 may 1959
wiener symphoniker/christoph von dohnanyi
lp: philips fontana 698 040CL/875 024CY/
SCFL 133/epic (usa) LC 3677

recorded in london watford town hall between
22-25 september 1966
london symphony orchestra/colin davis
lp: philips 802 764LY/802 878LY/SAL 3740/
AXS 12000/C75-AX200/6717 001/6747 375
cd: philips 454 3522/456 8232/
decca (korea) DN 0021

mozart/**piano concerto in f K459**

recorded in vienna konzerthaus between 22-26 june 1957
wiener symphoniker/carl melles
lp: vox PL 11010/STPL 511010/
GBY 11790/VBX 111
cd: allegretto ACD 8011
orchestra described on this recording as vienna pro musica

recorded in london walthamstow assembly hall between 2-5 december 1961
london symphony orchestra/colin davis
lp: philips fontana 698 081CL/875 061CY/
philips G03211L/837 051GY/GL 5813/
SGL 5813/610 802VL/838 602VY

recorded in london wembley town hall on 6-7 january 1966
london symphony orchestra/witold rowicki
lp: philips 802 879LY/SAL 3754/AXS 12000/
C75-AX200/6570 077/6717 001/6747 375
cd: philips 454 3522/decca (korea) DN 0021

piano concerto in d minor K466

recorded in vienna konzerthaus between 22-26 june 1957
wiener symphoniker/carl melles
lp: vox PL 11010/STPL 511010/
GBY 11790/VBX 111
cd: allegretto ACD 8011
orchestra described on this recording as vienna pro musica

recorded in london wembley town hall between 31 december 1965-2 january 1966
london symphony orchestra/alceo galliera
lp: philips 802 728LY/SAL 3626/BAL 30/
SBAL 30/AXS 12000/C71-AX402/
6580 008/6717 001/6747 375
cd: philips 450 0552/454 3522/
decca (korea) DN 0021

mozart/**piano concerto in c K467**

recorded in london wembley town hall between 9-13 january 1968
london symphony orchestra/witold rowicki
lp: philips 802 879LY/SAL 3754/AXS 12000/ C75-AX200/6527 147/6570 077/6580 083/ 6717 001/6747 375/420 0301
cd: philips 450 0552/454 3522/australian eloquence 468 1062/decca (korea) DN 0021

piano concerto in e flat K482

recorded in london watford town hall between 22-25 september 1966
london symphony orchestra/colin davis
lp: philips 802 764LY/802 878LY/SAL 3740/ AXS 12000/C75-AX200/6717 001/6747 375
cd: philips 454 3522/decca (korea) DN 0021

piano concerto in a K488

recorded in vienna konzerthaus between 22-26 june 1957
wiener symphoniker/paul walter
lp: vox PL 9830/GBY 11790/VBX 110
orchestra described on this recording as vienna pro musica

recorded in london wembley town hall between 4-6 january 1965
london symphony orchestra/witold rowicki
lp: philips A02438L/835 308LY/AL 3537/ SAL 3537/BAL 30/SBAL 30/AXS 1200/ C71-AX402/6580 008/6717 001/6747 375
cd: philips 454 3522/australian eloquence 468 1712/decca (korea) DN 0021

mozart/**piano concerto in c minor K491**

recorded in vienna konzerthaus on 7-8 may 1956
wiener symphoniker/paul walter
lp: vox PL 10080/GBY 10080/VBX 110
orchestra described on this recording as vienna pro musica

recorded in london walthamstow assembly hall on 3-4 may 1965
london symphony orchestra/colin davis
lp: philips 835 364AY/SAL 3642/AXS 12000/
6580 144/6717 001/6747 375
cd: philips 454 3522/australian eloquence 468 1712/
decca (korea) DN 0021

piano concerto in c K503

recorded in london wembley town hall between
20-22 august 1967
london symphony orchestra/alceo galliera
lp: philips 802 881LY/SAL 3718/AXS 12000/
C75-AX200/6717 001/6747 375
cd: philips 454 3522/decca (korea) DN 0021

mozart/**piano concerto in d K537 "coronation"**

recorded in vienna konzerthaus between 28-30 april 1955
wiener symphoniker/heinrich hollreiser
lp: vox PL 9390/GBY 12070/VBX 110
orchestra described on this recording as vienna pro musica

recorded in london walthamstow assembly hall between 2-5 december 1961
london symphony orchestra/colin davis
lp: philips fontana 698 081CL/875 061CY/philips G03211L/837 051GY/GL 5813/SGL 5813/ 663 036ER/610 802VL/838 602VY

recorded in london watford town hall between 6-11 november 1967
london symphony orchestra/witold rowicki
lp: philips 802 874LY/SAL 3753/AXS 12000/ 6527 147/6570 144/6580 043/6717 001/6747 375
cd: philips 422 9752/454 3522/ decca (korea) DN 0021

mozart/**piano concerto in b flat K595**

recorded in vienna konzerthaus on 25 march 1954
wiener symphoniker/heinrich hollreiser
lp: vox PL 8710/VBX 110
orchestra described on this recording as vienna pro musica

recorded in vienna musikvereinssaal between 9-11 may 1959
wiener symphoniker/christoph von dohnanyi
lp: philips fontana 698 040CL/875 034CY/
SCFL 133/philips 663 026ER/epic (usa) LC 3677

recorded in london wembley town hall between
31 december 1965-2 january 1966
london symphony orchestra/alceo galliera
lp: philips 802 728LY/SAL 3626/BAL 30/SBAL 30/
AXS 12000/C71-AX402/6717 001/6747 375
cd: philips 422 9752/454 3522/
decca (korea) DN 0021

rondo in d for piano and orchestra K382

recorded in london wembley town hall between
20-22 august 1967
london symphony orchestra/alceo galliera
lp: philips 802 881LY/SAL 3718/AXS 12000/
C75-AX200/6717 001/6747 375
cd: philips 452 3522/australian eloquence
468 1712/decca (korea) DN 0021

mozart/**rondo in a for piano and orchestra K386**

recorded in amsterdam concertgebouw on 7 july 1960
netherlands chamber orchestra/szymon goldberg
lp: philips fontana 698 059CL/875 040CY/
875 052CY
cd: retrospective 93407

recorded in london wembley town hall between
20-22 august 1967
london symphony orchestra/alceo galliera
lp: philips 802 881LY/SAL 3718/AXS 12000/
C75-AX200/6717 001/6747 375
cd: philips 452 3522/australian eloquence
468 1712/decca (korea) DN 0021

piano sonata in c K279

recorded in amsterdam bachzaal in june 1967
lp: philips 802 827LY/839 766LY/SAL 3666/
C71-AX601/6747 380/420 2921
cd: philips 456 1322/decca (korea) DN 0021/
tower records (japan) PROC 1201-1205

recorded in neumarkt reitstadel between 20-25 july 1989
cd: denon CO 76589/CO 76689/CO 79426-79430

piano sonata in f K280

recorded in amsterdam bachzaal in november 1965
lp: philips A02508L/835 378DXY/839 767LY/
C71-AX601/6747 380/420 2921
cd: philips 456 1322/decca (korea) DN 0021/
tower records (japan) PROC 1201-1205

recorded in neumarkt reitstadel between 25-31 october 1988
cd: denon CO 73202/CO 76689/CO 79426-79430

mozart/**piano sonata in b flat K281**

recorded in amsterdam bachzaal in november 1965
lp: philips A02508L/835 378DXY/839 757LY/
C71-AX601/6747 380/420 2921
cd: philips 456 1322/denon (korea) DN 0021/
tower records (japan) PROC 1201-1205

recorded in neumarkt reitstadel between 20-25 july 1989
cd: denon CO 76589/CO 76689/CO 79426-79430

piano sonata in e flat K282

recorded in amsterdam bachzaal in september 1963
lp: philips A02338L/835 216LY/839 765LY/
AL 3531/C71-AX601/6747 380/420 2921
cd: philips 456 1322/decca (korea) DN 0021/
tower records (japan) PROC 1201-1205

recorded in neumarkt reitstadel between 25-31 october 1988
cd: denon CO 73202/CO 76689/CO 79426-79430

piano sonata in g K283

recorded in amsterdam bachzaal in november 1965
lp: philips A02508L/835 378DXY/839 767LY/
C71-AX601/6747 380/420 2921
cd: philips 456 1322/decca (korea) DN 0021/
tower records (japan) PROC 1201-1205

recorded in neumarkt reitstadel between 20-25 july 1989
cd: denon CO 76589/CO 76689/CO 79426-79430

mozart/**piano sonata in d K284 "dürnitz"**

recorded in amsterdam bachzaal in june 1967
lp: philips 802 827LY/839 766LY/SAL 3666/
C71-AX601/6747 380/420 2921
cd: philips 456 1322/decca (korea) DN 0021/
tower records (japan) PROC 1201-1205

recorded in neustadt reitstadel between 16-21 july 1991
cd: denon CO 1848/CO 76689/CO 79426-79430

piano sonata in c K309

recorded in amsterdam bachzaal in december 1964
lp: philips A02440L/835 310AY/839 768LY/
C71-AX601/6747 380/420 2921
cd: philips 456 1322/decca (korea) DN 0021/
tower records (japan) PROC 1201-1205

recorded in neustadt reitstadel between 25-31 october 1988
cd: denon CO 73202/CO 76689/CO 79426-79430

piano sonata in a minor K310

recorded in amsterdam bachzaal in april 1963
lp: philips A02322L/839 764LY/C71-AX601/
6747 380/420 2921
cd: philips 456 1322/decca (korea) DN 0021/
tower records (japan) PROC 1201-1205

recorded in neustadt reitstadel between 1-8 august 1986
cd: denon CO 1517/CO 76689/CO 79426-79430

mozart/**piano sonata in d K311**

recorded in amsterdam bachzaal in april 1963
lp: philips A02322L/839 765LY/C71-AX601/
6747 380/420 2921
cd: philips 456 1322/decca (korea) DN 0021/
tower records (japan) PROC 1201-1205

recorded in neustadt reitstadel between 16-21 july 1991
cd: denon CO 76689/CO 79426-79430

piano sonata in c K330

recorded in amsterdam bachzaal in september 1963
lp: philips A02338L/835 216LY/839 765LY/
AL 3531/C71-AX601/6747 380/420 2921
cd: philips 456 1322/decca (korea) DN 0021/
tower records (japan) PROC 1201-1205

recorded in neustadt reitstadel between 1-8 august 1986
cd: denon CO 1517/CO 76689/CO 79426-79430

piano sonata in a K331

recorded in vienna and published in 1960
lp: vox GBY 12280

recorded in amsterdam bachzaal in april 1963
lp: philips A02332L/839 763LY/C71-AX601/
6747 380/420 2921
cd: philips 456 1322/decca (korea) DN 0021/
tower records (japan) PROC 1201-1205

recorded in neustadt reitstadel between 1-8 august 1986
cd: denon CO 1517/CO 76689/CO 79425-79430

mozart/**piano sonata in f K332**

recorded in amsterdam on 27-28 january 1954
lp: philips N00656R

recorded in amsterdam bachzaal in december 1964
lp: philips A02440L/835 310AY/839 768LY/
C71-AX601/6747 380/420 2921
cd: philips 456 1322/decca (korea) DN 0021/
tower records (japan) PROC 1201-1205

recorded in neustadt reitstadel between 1-8 august 1986
cd: denon CO 1848/CO 76689/CO 79426-79430

piano sonata in b flat K333

recorded in amsterdam on 27-28 january 1954
lp: philips N00656R

recorded in amsterdam bachzaal in june 1967
lp: philips 802 727LY/839 766LY/SAL 3666/
C71-AX601/6747 380/420 2921
cd: philips 456 1322/decca (korea) DN 0021/
tower records (japan) PROC 1201-1205

recorded in neustadt reitstadel between 1-8 august 1986
cd: denon CO 1848/CO 76689/CO 79426-79430

piano sonata in c minor K457

recorded in amsterdam concertgebouw on 1-3 july 1960
lp: philips fontana 698 026CL/802 749LY

recorded in amsterdam bachzaal in august 1966
lp: philips 839 764LY/C71-AX601/
6747 380/420 2921
cd: philips 456 1322/decca (korea) DN 0021/
tower records (japan) PROC 1201-1205

recorded in neustadt reitstadel between 12-16 january 1987
cd: denon CO 2195/CO 76689/CO 79426-79430

mozart/**piano sonata in f K533 and K494**

recorded in amsterdam bachzaal in august 1966
lp: philips 802 749LY/839 763LY/
C71-AX601/6747 380/420 2921
cd: philips 456 1322/decca (korea) DN 0021/
tower records (japan) PRC 1021-1025

recorded in neustadt reitstadel between 21-27 april 1987
cd: denon 72087/CO 76689/CO 79426-79430

piano sonata in c K545 "sonata facile"

recorded in amsterdam bachzaal in november 1965
lp: philips A02508L/835 378DXY/839 767LY/
C71-AX601/6747 380/420 2921
cd: philips 456 1322/decca (korea) DN 0021/
tower records (japan) PROC 1201-1205

recorded in neustadt reitstadel between 21-27 april 1987
cd: denon CO 72087/CO 76689/CO 79426-79430

piano sonata in b flat K570

recorded in amsterdam bachzaal in december 1964
lp: philips A02440L/835 310AY/839 768LY/
C71-AX601/6747 380/420 2021
cd: philips 456 1322/decca (korea) DN 0021/
tower records (japan) PROC 1201-1205

recorded in neustadt reitstadel between 12-16 january 1987
cd: denon CO 2195/CO 76689/CO 79426-79430

mozart/**piano sonata in d K576**

recorded in amsterdam bachzaal in september 1963
lp: philips A02338L/835 216LY/839 765LY/
AL 3531/C71-AX601/6747 380/420 2921
cd: philips 456 1322/456 8232/decca (korea)
DN 0021/tower records (japan) PROC 1201-1205

recorded in neustadt reitstadel between 21-27 april 1987
cd: denon CO 73087/CO 76689/CO 79426-79430

fantasia in d minor K397

recorded in amsterdam bachzaal in august 1966
lp: philips 802 749LY/C71-AX601/6747 380
cd: philips 456 1322/decca (korea) DN 0021

fantasia in c minor K475

recorded in amsterdam concertgebouw in july 1960
lp: philips fontana 698 026CL/802 749LY

recorded in amsterdam bachzaal in august 1966
lp: philips 839 764LY/C71-AX601/6747 380
cd: philips 456 1322/decca (korea) DN 0021

rondo in d K485

recorded in vienna and published in 1960
lp: vox GBY 12280

recorded in amsterdam in august 1977
lp: philips 9500 501
cd: philips 422 5182/426 8922/456 1322/
decca (korea) DN 0021

rondo in a minor K511

recorded in amsterdam bachzaal in september 1963
lp: philips A02338L/835 216LY/AL 3531/
C71-AX601/6747 380
cd: philips 456 1322/decca (korea) DN 0021

mozart/**variations on the dutch song “laat ons juichen” K24; variations on the dutch song “wilhelmus van nassouwe” K25; variations on a minuet by j.c. fischer K179; variations on salieri’s “mio caro adone” K180; variations on “lison dormait” K264; variations on gretry’s “dieu d’amour” K352; variations on “la belle francoise” K353; variations on “je suis lindor” K354; variations on paisiello’s “salve tu domine” K398; variations on gluck’s “unser dummer pöbel meint” K455; variations in b flat K500; variations on schack’s “ein weib ist das herrlichste ding” K613**

recorded in amsterdam concertgebouw in december 1975
lp: philips 6703 075/6747 380
cd: philips 422 5182/426 8922/456 1322/
decca (korea) DN 0021

variations on “ah vous dirai-je maman” K265; variations on a minuet by duport K573

recorded in vienna and published in 1960
lp: vox GBY 12280

recorded in amsterdam concertgebouw in december 1975
lp: philips 6703 075/6747 380
cd: philips 422 5182/426 8922/456 1322/
456 8232 (duport)/decca (korea) DN 0021

mozart/***variations on sarti's "come un agnello" K460**

recorded in amsterdam in december 1989
cd: philips 422 5182/426 8922/456 1322

adagio in b minor K540

recorded in amsterdam in august 1977
lp: philips 6747 380/9500 501
cd: philips 422 5182/426 8922/456 1322/
decca (korea) DN 0021

***allegro in c K1b; allegro in c K1c; allegro in b flat K3; allegro in g minor K312; allegro in b flat K400**

recorded in amsterdam in december 1989
cd: philips 422 5182/426 8922/456 1322

***andante in c K1a**

recorded in amsterdam in december 1989
cd: philips 422 5182/425 8922/456 1322

***capriccio in c K395**

recorded in amsterdam in december 1989
cd: philips 422 5182/426 8922/456 1322

eine kleine gigue in g K574

recorded in amsterdam in august 1977
lp: philips 6747 380/9500 501
cd: philips 422 5182/426 8922/456 1322/
decca (korea) DN 0021

***suite K399; fugue in g minor K401**

recorded in amsterdam in december 1989
cd: philips 422 5182/426 8922/456 1322

haebler plays fortepiano in the groups of recordings marked with an asterisk* mozart/*klavierstück in c K5a; klavierstück in f K33b; kleiner trauermarsch in c minor K453a**

recorded in amsterdam in december 1989
cd: philips 422 5182/426 8922/456 1322

***minuet in f K1d; minuet in g K1e; minuet in c K1f; minuet in f K2; minuet in f K4; minuet in f K5; minuet in d K94**

recorded in amsterdam in dec ember 1989
cd: philips 422 5182/426 8922/456 1322

minuet in d K355

recorded in amsterdam in august 1977
lp: philips 6747 380/9500 501
cd: philips 422 5182/426 8922/456 1322/
decca (korea) DN 0021

***prelude and fugue in c K394**

recorded in amsterdam in december 1989
cd: philips 422 5182/426 8922/456 1322

sonatas for piano duet: in c K19d; in g K357; in b flat K358; in d K381

recorded in vienna and published in 1959
with ludwig hoffmann (second piano)
lp: vox DL 432/VBX 66/SVBX 566

recorded in amsterdam in march 1976
with ludwig hoffmann (second piano)
lp: philips 802 817LY/6703 088/6747 380
cd: philips 422 5162/426 8902/454 0262/
456 1322/decca (korea) DN 0021

haebler plays fortepiano in the groups of recordings marked with an asterisk* mozart/sonata in f for piano duet K497; sonata in c for piano duet K521; andante with 5 variations in g for piano duet K501**

recorded in vienna and published in 1959
with ludwig hoffmann (second piano)
lp: vox DL 432/VBX 66/SVBX 566

recorded in amsterdam in december 1977
with ludwig hoffmann (second piano)
lp: philips 6703 088/6747 380
cd: philips 422 5162/426 8902/454 0262/
456 1322/decca (korea) DN 0021

sonata in d for two pianos K448; fugue in c minor for two pianos K426

recorded in la chaux de fonds in february 1978
with ludwig hoffmann (second piano)
lp: philips 6703 088/6747 380
cd: philips 422 5162/426 8902/454 0262/
456 1322/decca (korea) DN 0021

piano quartets in g minor K478 and e flat K493

recorded in vienna and published in 1959
with wolfgang poduschka (violin), helmut weis (viola) and otto blecha (cello)
lp: vox DL 740

recorded in berlin johannesstift between 1-4 april 1970
with michel schwalbe (violin), giusto cappone (viola) and ottomar borwitzky (cello)
lp: philips 6500 098/6747 383
cd: philips 420 8682/tower records (japan)
PROC 1223/decca (korea) DN 0021

mozart/**quintet for piano and wind in e flat K452**

recorded in salzburg mozarteum between 19-22 september 1971
with members of the bamberger symphoniker
lp: philips 6500 326/6747 383
cd: decca (korea) DN 0021

violin sonatas in c K296 and in e minor K304

recorded in salzburg mozarteum between 12-22 september 1969
with henryk szeryng (violin)
lp: philips 6500 053/6747 381
cd: philips 416 9022/decca (korea) DN 0021

violin sonata in g K301

recorded in salzburg mozarteum between 4-8 january 1972
with henryk szeryng (violin)
lp: philips 6500 143/6747 381
cd: philips 416 9022/decca (korea) DN 0021

violin sonata in e flat K302

recorded in salzburg mozarteum between 16-19 may 1972
with henryk szeryng (violin)
lp: philips 6500 145/6747 381
cd: philips 416 9022/decca (korea) DN 0021

mozart/**violin sonata in c K303**

recorded in salzburg mozarteum between
1-3 september 1972
with henryk szeryng (violin)
lp: philips 6500 145/6747 391
cd: philips 416 9022/decca (korea) DN 0021

violin sonata in a K305

recorded in salzburg mozarteum between
12-22 september 1969
with henryk szeryng (violin)
lp: philips 6500 143/6747 381
cd: philips 416 9022/decca (korea) DN 0021

violin sonata in d K306

recorded in salzburg mozarteum between
1-3 september 1972
with henryk szeryng (violin)
lp: philips 6500 144/6747 381
cd: philips 416 9022/decca (korea) DN 0021

violin sonata in f K376

recorded in salzburg mozarteum between
4-8 january 1972
with henryk szeryng (violin)
lp: philips 6500 143/6747 381
cd: philips 416 9022/decca (korea) DN 0021

violin sonatas in f K377 and in f K378

recorded in salzburg mozarteum between
12-22 september 1969
with henryk szeryng (violin)
lp: philips 6500 054/6747 381
cd: philips 416 9022/decca (korea) DN 0021

mozart/**violin sonata in g K379**

recorded in salzburg mozarteum between
4-8 january 1972
with henryk szeryng (violin)
lp: philips 6500 143/6747 381
cd: philips 416 9022/decca (korea) DN 0021

violin sonata in e flat K380

recorded in salzburg mozarteum between
1-3 september 1972
with henryk szeryng (violin)
lp: philips 6500 144/6747 381
cd: philips 416 9022/decca (korea) DN 0021

violin sonatas in b flat K454
and in e flat K481

recorded in salzburg mozarteum between
12-22 september 1969
with henryk szeryng (violin)
lp: pjilips 6500 055/6747 381
cd: philips 416 9022/decca (korea) DN 0021

violin sonata in c K526

recorded in salzburg mozarteum between
12-22 september 1969
with henryk szeryng (violin)
lp: philips 6500 053/6747 381
cd: philips 416 9022/decca (korea) DN 0021

mozart/**violin sonata in f K547**

recorded in salzburg mozarteum between 16-19 may 1972
with henryk szeryng (violin)
lp: philips 6500 145/6747 381
cd: philips 416 9022/decca (korea) DN 0021

variations in g for violin and piano on "la bergere celimene" K359 and on "helas j'ai perdu mon amant" K360

recorded in salzburg mozarteum between 1-3 september 1972
with henryk szeryng (violin)
lp: philips 6500 145 (K359)/6500 144 (K360)/
6747 381
cd: philips 416 9022/decca (korea) DN 0021

FRANZ SCHUBERT (1797-1828)

piano sonatas in e D459 and in c minor D958

recorded in salzburg mozarteum in may 1970
lp: philips 6500 082/6741 002
cd: philips 456 3672/478 5859/
decca (korea) DN 0021

piano sonatas in a minor D537 and in a minor D845

recorded in berlin johannesstift in march 1970
lp: philips 6741 002
cd: philips 456 3672/478 5859/
decca (korea) DN 0021

schubert/**piano sonatas in e flat D568 and in b D575**

recorded in berlin johannesstift in november 1968
lp: philips 839 770LY/6741 002
cd: philips 456 3672/478 5859/
decca (korea) DN 0021

piano sonata in a D664

recorded in amsterdam bachzaal in april 1960
lp: philips fontana 698 039CL/802 738LY

recorded in salzburg mozarteum in february 1969
lp: philips A02493L/835 363AY/839 772LY/
AL 3604/SAL 3604/6741 002
cd: philips 456 3672/478 5859/
decca (korea) DN 0021

piano sonatas in a minor D784 and in b flat D960

recorded in eindhoven in october 1967
lp: philips 6741 002
cd: philips 456 3672/456 8232/478 5859/
decca (korea) DN 0021

piano sonata in d D850

recorded in salzburg mozarteum in february 1969
lp: philips 839 773LY/6741 002
cd: philips 456 3672/478 5859/
decca (korea) DN 0021

schubert/**piano sonata in g D894**

recorded in amsterdam bachzaal in april 1960
lp: philips fontana 698 050CL

recorded in salzburg mozarteum in february 1969
lp: philips A02493L/835 363AY/839 772LY/
AL 3604/SAL 3604/6741 002
cd: philips 456 3672/478 5859/
decca (korea) DN 0021

piano sonata in a D959

recorded in berlin johannessstift in november 1968
lp: philips 839 769LY/6741 002
cd: philips 456 3672/478 5859/
decca (korea) DN 0021

moments musicaux D780

recorded in amsterdam bachzaal in april 1960
lp: philips fontana 698 050CL/philips
802 738LY/SAL 3647
cd: philips 456 3672/478 5859/
decca (korea) DN 0021

the four impromptus D899

*recorded in vienna konzerthaus between
17-23 december 1954*
lp: vox PL 8940/STPL 58940

recorded in amsterdam concertgebouw in may 1963
lp: philips A02321L/610 150VL/412 0121
cd: philips 456 3672/478 5859/
decca (korea) DN 0021

undated recording by bbc manchester
unpublished radio broadcast

schubert/**the four impromptus D935**

recorded in vienna konzerthaus between
17-23 december 1954
lp: vox PL 8940/STPL 58940

recorded in amsterdam concertgebouw in may 1963
lp: philips A02321L/610 150VL/412 0121
cd: philips 456 3672/478 5859/
decca (korea) DN 0021

deutsche tänze D783

recorded in amsterdam bachzaal in april 1960
lp: philips fontana 698 039CL/
philips 802 738LY/SAL 3647
cd: philips 456 3672/478 5859/
decca (korea) DN 0021

fantasy in f minor for two pianos D940; introduction and variations on an original theme for two pianos D603; rondo for piano duet D608; two marches caracteristiques for two pianos D886

recorded in amsterdam bachzaal between
10-14 may 1961
with ludwig hoffmann (second piano)
lp: philips fontana 698 069CL/875 053CY/
philips 6530 063
cd: philips 456 3672/478 5859/
decca (korea) DN 0021

schubert/**piano quintet in d D667 "die forelle"**

recorded in amsterdam between 23-26 august 1966
with arthur grumiaux (violin), georges janzer (viola), eva czako (cello) and jacques cazauran (double-bass)
lp: philips 802 757LY/SAL 3621/6570 115
cd: philips 422 8382/decca (korea) DN 0021

three violin sonatinas: in D D344, in a minor D385 and in g minor D408

recorded between 23-26 july 1974
with henryk szeryng (violin)
lp: philips 6500 885

duo in a for violin and piano D574

recorded between 23-26 july 1974
with henryk szeryng (violin)
lp: philips 6500 885

ROBERT SCHUMANN (1810-1856)

papillons op 2

recorded in amsterdam concertgebouw in august 1959
lp: philips fontana 698 039CL
cd: philips 456 8232

kinderszenen op 15

recorded in amsterdam concertgebouw in august 1959
lp: philips fontana 698 039CL/
philips 802 738LY/SAL 3647
cd: philips 456 8232

john hunt

life with music

recollections of

an obsessive

Beginnings

On 20 June 1938 soprano Elisabeth Schwarzkopf was singing the small role of Esmeralda in Smetana's *The Bartered Bride* at Berlin's Charlottenburg Opera House (having debuted earlier that yeart as a Flower Maiden in Wagner's *Parsifal),* conductor Herbert von Karajan was back in his home town of Salzburg after a successful debut concert with the Berlin Philharmonic (he was due to make his first ever gramophone record at the end of the year), Maria Callas was about to enrol as a student in the Athens Conservatory and almost immediately undertake her first stage role as Santuzza in Mascagni's *Cavalleria Rusticana,* Wilhelm Furtwängler was preparing to conduct a series of performances of Wagner's *Tristan und Isolde* at the Paris Opera, and the young Russian pianist Sviatoslav Richter was working in Moscow as a repetiteur (where he had already prepared performances of Stravinsky's *Oedipus Rex).*

So that was how the five major interpretative artists who were to mould my musical perceptions were occupied on that June day when I entered the world at Windsor's Princess Christian Nursing Home (named after one of Queen Victoria's daughters). Of course it was not until I reached early adulthood that I would consciously start to come under any of these influences, before which there would be a random succession of chance musical experiences during my teenage years.

Fascinating to know as well that just weeks before my birth, a momentous musical event was taking place much nearer home in London's Queens Hall and preserved on a recording: the renowned Italian maestro Arturo Toscanini was conducting Verdi's *Messa da Requiem.*

By however small a margin, I feel tremendously privileged to have been born in those inter-war years and feel more than a close affinity with the history, both musical and otherwise, that enrolled in Western Europe during that era. For the moment, however, let me sketch in those random discoveries which I feel must have set me on the path of my particular lifelong obsession.

Opposite page: John Hunt drawn in 1993 by Philip Boardman

My mother Susan Ann Young was a true Londoner, possessing a facility at the piano (although completely untrained) for which she sadly had little time as I, her firstborn, was followed between 1941 and 1950 by a brother Robert and two sisters, Julie and Anna. My father, Reginald Charles Peter, was a traditional jazz and football aficionado who seemed disappointed that I showed no sign of sharing his passions. From his side of the family, however, I did eventually acquire two cousins, Malcolm and Alison, who pursued careers as composer and folk-singer respectively.

What I vividly remember in my paternal grandmother's home was a wind-up gramophone with cabinet underneath containing assorted discs: I was particularly fascinated, and repeatedly played, those containing music from Bizet's *L'Arlesienne* played by Sir Thomas Beecham and the London Philharmonic Orchestra, probably without even realising that the pieces added up to an integral suite! This encouraged me eventually to visit a music shop on Windsor's Castle Hill (I think it was called Dyson's – it resembled more a hardware shop) in order to purchase the shellac discs making up Tchaikovsky's First Piano Concerto (this was an HMV version by pianist Artur Rubinstein with the London Symphony Orchestra conducted by Sir John Barbirolli).

Due to my father's work as a sales representative for the ICI paint firm, we left Windsor in 1950 for Sale in Cheshire (a suburb of Manchester) and eventually Tynemouth on the bracing North-East coast (we had already endured one three-year period of exile during the war, whilst my father was overseas with the armed forces). The North-East was not to my taste (always bitterly cold, it seemed), and I took every opportunity, during school holidays, to come back to Windsor to stay with my two aunts or grandmother. My mother, on the other hand, fitted well in her new Northern environment and made several good friends there as her relationship with my father worsened.

What I do have to thank the North-East for, as well as my time at Tynemouth High School, is my introduction to the world of the German Language and that of concert-going. I had originally chosen to pursue Commercial Art as an A-level subject, but for some reason made a last-minute change to Modern Languages (primarily German). We were a co-educational school, where most of the boys opted for Science and Mathematics, so that I found myself in a class of highly competitive girls, which spurred me out of any laziness. And in Marjorie Worswick I had a nonpareil German tutor, with whom I seemed to be very much on the same wavelength (I also had to take extra private tuition in Latin, as that was also an A-level requirement in those days for those who wanted to consider entering university in order to study modern languages). The twin trauma of not being good at either Mathematics or any sports, which I absolutely hated, were soon behind me. I also recall, at about the age of fourteen, falling in love with a girl who was singing the part of Hansel in a school production of *Hänsel und Gretel,* although of formal music lessons at school I recall not one iota!

Having seen film adaptations of Verdi's *Rigoletto* and Gounod's *Faust* in a local cinema, my first taste of opera on stage was encountering Wagner's *Tannhäuser* which the Carl Rosa Company put on at Newcastle's Theatre Royal (it must have been around 1953); whilst at the City Hall in Newcastle, which was only a twenty-minute train ride from Tynemouth, I gradually started to attend concerts by the Halle Orchestra (including one of the first performances of Vaughan Williams' Eighth Symphony under Barbirolli), the long since defunct Yorkshire Symphony Orchestra and even the Israel Philharmonic Orchestra under Paul Paray. An interest in different performances of the same work had already been sparked whilst listening to the BBC Third Programme (while supposed to be doing my homework), who presented a series of the Beethoven Symphonies in recorded versions by both Toscanini and Weingartner.

On one of my summer holidays in Windsor, I ventured up to London to a Henry Wood Promenade Concert at the Royal Albert Hall (Sir Malcolm Sargent conducted music by Elgar and Holst), although strangely enough it would not be until my retirement years that the Proms would become a regular part of my concert-going life.

One final recollection of those formative years was spending time at the home of a school friend, whose mother coached (actually mesmerised) me into passing O-level Mathematics and whose older brother had some very modern hi-fi equipment and new long-playing discs which were such an advance on the old shellac ones I had been used to: I particularly remember being impressed by the power of an HMV record of William Walton's First Symphony conducted by the composer.

My very first encounter with the German-speaking world was not a musical one. Having worked on its language and literature for a few years at school, I was sent in the summer of 1955 on an exchange visit to stay with a family in the Rhineland town of Neuss. It was a hard test for a seventeen year-old with no practical experience of speaking the language, as the family themselves spoke a dialect of *Plattdeutsch* far removed from the schoolroom High German which I knew. However, I formed a good friendship with Paul Janssen, and returned for several summers, even taking holiday jobs in German factories. Paul in turn visited my family in the North-East of England, and we remained good friends until well into the 1980s.

Germany in 1955 was still very much scarred by the devastation of the world war which had ended in defeat only a decade earlier, with ruined buildings much in evidence – some still bearing slogans daubed on them by the Nazi authotrities in order to encourage the people in their war effort. Despite the warnings of my grandmother about the atrocities committed, I was eager to see things for myself and encountered nothing but open friendliness, albeit with the occasional reserve towards foreigners.

As I went on in subsequent years to discover other parts of Germany, usually with musical encounters built in, I became aware of my affinity with the country and its people, even feeling, when I eventually reached as far as Berlin and Dresden, that I may in a former life have been there before. For the moment it is back to London where I had resolved to enrol at University College to broaden my encounter with the language and literature of the country which I already admired so much.

Visiting the capital earlier in 1956 for my university application interview, I lost no time in visiting the Royal Festival Hall, then only five years old since its 1951 opening for the Festival of Britain. It seemed like a mecca with its posters advertising events with musicians from all over the world. Sadly the hall was not really living up to its builders' claims that it would replace the renowned Queens Hall (destroyed during the Second War), although it was not until later, and with experience of the great European concert and opera venues, that I would really become aware of its acoustic deficiencies – it did not, for example, flatter a warm and refulgent string tone. None of that has prevented me from chalking up a total number of 1396 performances attended at the hall and its two satellites (Queen Elizabeth Hall and Purcell Room), whilst over the Thames at the Royal Opera House I have heard 677 performances and recitals, most of them playing a very important part in forming my musical tastes.

Concert-going started in earnest once I had enrolled at University College in the autumn of 1956, and as booking tickets mainly involved regular monthly (at Covent Garden bi-monthly) queuing, one formed many acquaintanceships, even friendships, with fellow enthusiasts. Among them, for example, was Yvonne Pegler, whose father had been a supplying contractor when the hall was being built, and who to this day occupies a fixed position in the front stalls at almost all concerts (her tally of performances exceeds mine many times over!). The biggest queues, overnight ones in fact, were when Maria Callas gave Royal Festival Hall recitals with orchestra, or when she and other stars appeared in opera at Covent Garden. At that venue, bringing an overnight sleeping bag was of limited avail, encamped as one was in the middle of a busy fruit and vegetable market with little chance of real sleep!

That first London season of orchestral concerts had for me as its highlights performances from the Philharmonia Orchestra, who seemed to possess a seriousness and cultivated high quality which was rivalled by its competitors, the London Philharmonic and BBC Symphony Orchestras, only intermittently. Perhaps Philharmonia's nearest rival was Sir Thomas Beecham's Royal Philharmonic Orchestra, whose concerts both at the Royal Festival and Royal Albert Halls, always generated a marvellous sense of occasion, of being special. It was Beecham who, dismayed by the mediocre quality of the music-making of his colleagues, came out with the dictum that the British public does not understand music but only the noise that it makes! I am afraid that Beecham's barbed comment was, in my subsequent experience, very close to the mark.

And now, to conclude this introduction, the first of what will be more than a few gripes in the course of these pages. In the 1950s and through to the 1970s a visit to London's Royal Festival Hall was for a concert and perhaps a coffee afterwards, over which one might discuss the concert with friends. The esteemed critic Neville Cardus might be seen there penning his review for the Manchester Guardian. If I remember rightly, there was a segregated (and expensive) restaurant upstairs, otherwise it was a peaceful haven. Then some liberal-minded planners from the London County Council decided that the building should become an open house, with access to all and sundry during the day. Gradually the Hall and its environs became filled with souvenir shops, food outlets, street musicians and mothers breast-feeding their babies, to name just a few of the "attractions" through which one has nowadays to fight one's way to get to the concert. How I cherish my visits to venues on the continent of Europe, where I can attend a concert experience without such unwelcome diversions!

1957-1958

For the final segment of that first academic year in the German department of University College London, we students were required to spend the summer term at a university of individual choice in the German-speaking countries. The majority of my colleagues (some of whom seemed to value the social benefits of being at university more highly than the academic ones) opted for the most popular venues like Munich, Bonn, Heidelberg or Frankfurt. Ever the loner, I chose somewhere less well-known, where I might not be surrounded by other English speakers and therefore able to progress quickly to a more respectable command of the German language. It turned out that only one other English student (from Kings College London) had enrolled at the university of Würzburg, and whilst we became good friends we did discipline ourselves to speak German almost exclusively.

The town of Würzburg, located in that region of Northern Bavaria known as Franconia, lies like a jewel in a landscape of great beauty of both nature and architecture, and readers of my generation may recall that the historian Kenneth Clark devoted time, in his television series "Civilisation: a personal view", to extolling the area, not just the magnicient Würzburg Residenz with its Tiepolo ceilings but the pilgrimage churches like Vierzehnheiligen. A Mozart Festival was held each summer in the Residenz (I recall one special concert by the Sinfonieorchester des Bayerischen Rundfunks under conductor Eugen Jochum). Although the town's original opera house (where one Richard Wagner had held his very first professional conducting appointment) had been razed to the ground by allied bombs during the second war, a temporary edifice was in use in 1957, and it was there that I heard the first of my 42 (to date) performances of the Richard Strauss comedy for music known as *Der Rosenkavalier*. However, that Würzburg sojourn proved to be a mere stepping stone to something far more significant to me.

Unbelievable as it may seem today, tickets were still freely available only weeks before the performances at the Bayreuth Festival, and so in the first week of August 1957 we took a local train further across the Franconian countryside to the town where Richard Wagner had set up his own festival and where, for the sixth successive year since its post-war reopening, performances were in full swing. In 1951 *Die Meistersinger von Nürnberg* had been presented in a traditional version, but now the composer's grandson Wieland had staged it in what was, for the conservative mainstream audience, a spare but colourful re-interpretation. For me, it was the combination of Bayreuth's unique acoustical properties and the tangible atmosphere of the place where Wagnerian performance history had been unravelling for 80 years which determined that I would come back, bi-annually as it turned out, for the next 50.

Later in that same month a visit to another European music centre beckoned for a party of students, which I was lucky enough to join. The best way in which I can describe the impact on me of that first visit to Salzburg is to enumerate the performances which I attended within a single week (conductor and principle singers are given) :-
19 august 1957/Strauss *Elektra*
Mitropoulos/Borkh/Madeira/Della Casa/Lorenz/Böhme
21 August 1957/Verdi *Falstaff*
Karajan/Schwarzkopf/Simionato/Moffo/Zampieri/Gobbi/Panerai
22 August 1957/Brahms *Ein deutsches Requiem*
Karajan/Della Casa/Fischer-Dieskau
24 August 1957/Mozart *Le nozze di Figaro*
Böhm/Schwarzkopf/Seefried/Ludwig/Kunz/Fischer-Dieskau
25 August 1957/Mozart *Die Entführung aus dem Serail*
Conz/Köth/Otto/Gedda/Dickie/Böhme
The performance of the Brahms *Requiem* was literally overheard from the open windows of the student hostel where we were accommodated, situated high on the *Mönchsberg* hill overlooking the *Felsenreitschulr* concert venue (in those days this was still an open-air structure, so that if weather conditions were unfavourable the performance would have to be transferred to the *Festspielhaus).*

This cornucopia of musical riches was to set me up for 33 consecutive years of visits to the idyllic city of Salzburg, and yet by the time I was back for my second visit in the summer of 1958 with another mouth-watering programme of concentrated operatic and concert delights, another landmark event had already struck back in London: this was my first encounter with the operatic phenomenon that was Maria Callas!

My friend Maisie Woodard and I were in the habit of jointly marking our birthdays, ehich fell on consecutive days (19 and 20 June), and in 1958 she had secured tickets for us for a Festival Hall concert by the London Mozart Players (19 June) and the Covent Garden revival of Verdi's *La traviata* in which Callas would be starring (20 June). I could hardly anticipated that I would be celebrating my twentieth birthday with hearing such a perfect realisation of an Italian operatic masterpiece, and can honestly say that none of the 17 subsequent stage performances of that opera which I have attended has approached that first one in its all-embracing honesty and emotional power, qualities which only sporadically come to the fore in many routine versions. The surviving BBC recording of that Covent Garden evening could almost be taken to typify the Callas qualities of penetrating to the heart of a composer's groundplan, and of bringing stock operatic situations to new and pulsating life. To anyone who might be sceptical about the importance of Maria Callas I would strongly recommend listening to this recording, or perhaps to one of her studio recordings of pieces like Puccini's *La boheme* or Leoncavallo's *I pagliacci*: for it is ironically enough in roles to which one might think Callas temperamentally less suited that her skill at entering the heart of such characters reveals itself most distinctively.

In the next 6 years, which incidentally turned out to be the last ones for Callas as a regular stage performer, I seized every possible chance of attending her London appearances, including Cherubini's *Medea* (2 times), Puccini's *Tosca* (3 times) and 3 separate Royal Festival Hall recitals with orchestra. Then in 1973, that much discussed (and, I feel, much misunderstood) comeback recital which for her fans was an unforgettable evening of homage to the diva of the twentieth century. I cannot claim to have known Maria Callas personally (although she did once speak on my telephone), but a good friend of mine, Jose Luis Luna, did, and it was his enthusiasm which helped bring me ever closer to the world of this complex musical figure. She became one of the 5 interpreters who formed my musical pantheon.

Walter Legge

Having graduated from London University and subsequently decided that I was not cut out to be a schoolteacher, I decided to try and find employment in that world of music which was by now occupying so much of my spare time anyway. EMI was advertising for an assistant in its Progress Department based at the Hayes Record Factory, which involved charting and coercing of the many stages of LP record manufacture, starting with editing and approval of tapes and continuing through the various factory stages of producing final test pressings: these in turn needed to be submitted back to the recording producer (representing the artists who had participated) for final approval before the LP could be mass-produced and put out on the market. Our work covered both the popular and classical record labels which by this time came under EMI's vast umbrella. It would be fair to say that a good 80 per cent of the work ran smoothly, with target dates being met and the LPs reaching the shops for the scheduled release dates: the exception was the Columbia classical label, which because of its high levels of artistic integrity under its main producer Walter Legge had, by the late 1950s, overtaken HMV in reputation. Behind the scenes there would be battles, with Legge requiring endless re-cutting of the LP sides until they reached his ideal sound quality. It meant that Columbia LPs were often late in reaching the shops, nor was there any guarantee that the standard monaural versions of a disc and the concurrent edition in the emerging stereophonic format would reach the market at the same time. The very first stereophonic LPs which I recall buying under the staff purchase scheme (with discount) were, I recall, delayed until several months after the mono version had appeared: these were Mozart's *Don Giovanni* recorded under the baton of Carlo Maria Giulin

To describe Walter Legge as concert promoter and classical record producer is something of an understatement: for 4 out of the 5 performing musicians who formed my musical pantheon, he was the artistic umbrella under which, at varying stages of their respective careers, these artists were enabled to display their interpretative gifts. Whilst Legge did not actually create Callas, Schwarzkopf, Furtwängler and Karajan (what he did create, in 1945 and out of a fragmented and war-torn Britain, was the Philharmonia Orchestra), he nevertheless provided them with the ideal conditions, mainly in the recording studio but sometimes also in the actual concerts which he promoted, needed to realise their innate potential.

At EMI Legge had at his disposal a loyal team of technical and secretarial assistants, with whom the likes of the Hayes staff would liaise, and it was not until over a decade later (by which time he was in virtual retirement, aside from managing the concert career of his wife Elisabeth Schwarzkopf) that I had an actual opportunity to meet with him at length in what was a sort of retrospective discussion. With a little flattery and, I recall, a few brandies, he helped me fill many gaps in my knowledge. I certainly already knew about his early EMI years, first as programme annotator and assistant to the legendary Fred Gaisberg, his own first independent producing assignments for the Hugo Wolf Society (recordings appeared on the HMV label) and concurrent work with Sir Thomas Beecham (published on the Columbia label – I have already mentioned the excerpts from Bizet's *L'Arlesienne,* one of the many titles which had graced Columbia's catalogue in the late 30s). Culmination of this work was the production of Mozart's *Die Zauberflöte* set up for Beecham to conduct in Berlin in 1937 (much to the chagrin of Fritz Busch and Glyndebourne, who felt that their pioneering records of the 3 Mozart-Da Ponte operas would earn them the right to record *Zauberflöte* as well!) Politics was of course no longer to be ignored in 1937 Germany, and the (Jewish) Legge, with Beecham at his side, had to accept several Nazi Party members in important cast roles for this recording as the price for having the eminent Berliner Philharmonisches Orchester participating, as opposed to the likes of Richard Tauber and Alexander Kipnis who might otherwise have been first choice. *Zauberflöte* was also an opera to which Walter Legge would return on two more occasions in the recording studio, under conductors Herbert von Karajan (1951) and Otto Klemperer (1961), and all 3 are, in my view and despite being shorn of the problematic spoken dialogue, benchmark recordings of the work.

The other branch of Legge's activities which I was lucky enough to experience at close quarters was his promotion of the Philharmonia Orchestra's concert series. Aside from the satisfying musical content, with a roster of conducting talent drawn not only from those who made records for Columbia and HMV but also from the wider international community, these programmes contributed to maintaining the highest standards at London's Royal Festival Hall; they also embraced song recitals by the leading Lieder interpreters of the period, Legge's wife Elisabeth Schwarzkopf, Irmgard Seefried and Dietrich Fischer-Dieskau. Musical content was matched in all cases by accompanying programme books of a scholarly standard unmatched by any of the other concert promoters active at that time. My collection of these distinctive publications remain some of my prized possessions which document a very special era: it was so special that when, in the mid 60s pressure came from the Greater London Council, itself responsible for running the Royal Festival Hall, for all orchestras and their promoters to conform to guidelines designed to co-ordinate and rationalise their activities, Legge decided to throw in the towel and disband the Philharmonia Orchestra. To its credit the orchestra re-formed under its own management: for some years it partially upheld the old standards (not least with loyal help from its conductors Otto Klemperer, Carlo Maria Giulini and Lorin Maazel), but ultimately an era was at an end.

Walter Legge was a *grand seigneur* in a changing world – he viewed his colleagues at EMI (Victor Olof and Peter Andry on the HMV branch) with some disdain, whilst a member of his own production staff, the Indian-born Suvi Raj Grubb, was referred to as "Monostatos" (the somewhat suspect character of dark skin in Mozart's *Zauberflöte).* Legge's days were numbered as standardisation and dumbing down crept into the music business, and I feel that he was perfectly justified in pulling the plug on a musical flagship which he had created back in 1945 in order to combat those very symptoms of mediocrity.

In the 1930s and right up to the mid 1950s, complete sets of a composer's output (or one branch of it) were the exception rather than the rule. The young Legge was still a junior figure as HMV made its first steps towards completism with its Hugo Wolf Lieder or Sibelius symphony projects, moving on to an integral set of the Beethoven Piano Sonatas from the reluctant Artur Schnabel. Not until post-war and the LP era was Legge able to realise not one but two complete Beethoven Symphony sets (Karajan and Klemperer), but what is not always fully realised is that he also fully committed to aiming for LP sets of the Piano concerti and sonatas with the likes of Claudio Arrau, Walter Gieseking and Hans Richter-Haaser (not to mention dozens of individual versions from that repertoire with pianists like Egon Petri, Artur Schnabel, Denis Matthews, Solomon, Geza Anda, Edwin Fischer, Emil Gilels and Moiseiwitsch).

Details of the above recordings, and everything else, are contained in the Walter Legge discography compliled by Alan Sanders and published by Greenwood Press back in 1984. Later Alan also edited a highly illuminating selection of Legge's writings under the title "Words and Music" (published by Duckworth). And in an antiquarian bookshop only recently I came across programme books of wartime ENSA concerts which Legge had organised and to which he often contributed astute programme notes. From the "Words and Music" compendium I would singly out the obituary tribute to the great horn player Dennis Brain, which demonstrates not only Legge's unsurpassed qualities as an music connoisseur but also as a sensitive and charitable friend to the artists under his supervision.

Her master's voice

The undoubted highlight of my very first season of Festival Hall concerts, promoted by Walter Legge's Philharmonia Concert Society, was a Sunday afternoon recital of Lieder by Hugo Wolf, the composer whom Legge had championed above all others. And for a near perfect interpreter of these songs he had to look no further than his wife.

In a singing career lasting a full 41 years, Elisabeth Schwarzkopf appeared in public 2404 times, 850 of these in Lieder recitals, 400 in choral and orchestral concerts and a staggering 1154 times on the operatic stage! Added to which was a gruelling schedule of recording sessions, revealing all in all a workload which would seem inconceivable to today's singers.

Naturally I was able to experience only a tiny proportion of this remarkable achievement, but was lucky enough to enjoy at first hand some of the great moments of the Schwarzkopf career, as she concentrated more on the recital stage whilst restricting her operatic roles (3 of Mozart and 2 of Richard Strauss) in a process of continual refinement. Her very entrance onto the platform of the Royal Festival Hall aroused an anticipation among the audience that we were to experience, indeed enjoy, something really special.

It was not until the years of her retirement and her new active role as a teacher that I seized the opportunity to make the acquaintance of the (by now) Dame Elisabeth. There soon came the chance to become involved in the formation of the Elisabeth Schwarzkopf-Walter Legge Society, which would promote interest in the vital work carried out for music by this remarkable partnership. I had hoped that this would become something more than just another fan club. Unfortunately, having set in motion a plan to mark the tenth anniversary of Legge's death with a piano recital by none other than Sviatoslav

Richter, the Society was commandeered by a group of extremely possessive lesbians, whose fawning admiration actually resulted in Dame Elisabeth reducing her teaching activities in the UK and concentrating instead on mainland Europe and the USA.

However, we remained on good terms, and Dame Elisabeth continued to show an interest in my discographic work, to the extent of actually making a financial contribution. Sadly her last years were blighted by a spiteful attack from one Alan Jefferson in a so-called biography of the singer: this vilified her for having pursued her early career against a backdrop of political intrigue (part of the wave of political correctness which has since come to pervade every area of our society). Jefferson had apparently once been a *confidant* of Legge but they had fallen out, and this may have been his way of seeking revenge? In preparing his very poorly researched project Jefferson had gained the confidence of many interested parties, including myself, and then published our names in an acknowledgement. Dame Elisabeth naturally thought that we had known in advance what would be the tenor of Jefferson's argument, and it was my great regret that I never had the opportunity to refute this and convince her that I was one hundred per cent on her side. As a result of such attacks, she herself had adopted a defensive stance (perfectly justified, I would say) about her alleged involvement with the Nazi hierarchy during those apprentice years at Berlin's Charlottenburg Opera House.

As we observed in her work in the public masterclasses, Dame Elisabeth could be harsh when students were not sufficiently prepared. But then I recall the occasion when a young soprano, who was the daughter of two famous film stars, gave an unblemished account of the Marschallin's monologue from *Der Rosenkavalier* which left the teacher

Opposite page: John Hunt with Dame Elisabeth Schwarzkopf in 1985 speechless with admiration. On quite a different occasion she admonished me for having made some sweeping statement, but almost immediately apologised for having dismissed me so abruptly. Schwarzkopf and I had for one short concurrent period (1960-1963) worked for the same company, and as an afterthought I even got to deputise for her when the Richard Tauber Foundation asked me to be involved in a showing of Tauber's *Pagliacci* film at London's Queen Elizabeth Hall.

In performances of Mozart's *Don Giovanni* it has seemed to me that the character of Donna Elvira is often reduced to an undignified (hysterical) victim of Giovanni, in contrast to the strong-minded Donna Anna. With Elisabeth Schwarzkopf as Elvira this was never the case: critic Neville Cardus remarked back in 1959, after a concert performance of the opera in the Royal Festival Hall, that Giovanni would surely never have tired of a woman of such beauty and of such radiant personality. And yet the real essence of Schwarzkopf the singer is to be found in her Lieder performances. I would recommend to the inquisitive younger reader that he samples one of the many live recordings, preferably complete recitals, now available to us: for example a Schubert evening from Salzburg in 1960 (Orfeo CD C826 103D) or the Festival Hall programme in 1968 with songs by Wolf, Schubert and Strauss and dedicated to the memory of Walter Legge's mentor Ernest Newman (Eklipse CD EKRP 4).

I count myself more than lucky to have been at 44 of those remarkable recitals between 1957 and 1978 in the Royal Festival Hall (22), Goldsmiths Hall (1), BBC Broadcasting House (1), Bath Assembly Rooms (1), Chichester Festival Theatre (1)), Elstree Haberdashers School (1), Windsor Castle Waterlo Chamber (1), Brighton Dome (1), Camden Town Hall (3), Croydon Fairfield Halls (2), Sutton Granada Cinema (1), Eastbourne Congress Theatre (1), Royal Opera House Covent Garden (2) and the Wigmore Hall (5)

Philharmonic autocrat

Those Salzburg Festival appearances in 1957-1958 (actually the first since Herbert von Karajan had taken over as the Festival's artistic director), the first Berlin Philharmonic Orchestra visit to London with him in 1958 and three concerts with the Philharmonia Orchestra (his very last with that orchestra): all these formed my introduction to the most remarkable conducting figure of the twentieth century's second half. This was music-making of a quality not previously encountered by me. The single-minded unanimity of the double basses' sweep in Beethoven's Fifth Symphony, the incandescent glow in Wagner's *Meistersinger* overture or *Tristan* prelude or the luminous penetration of Strauss' *Tod und Verklärung,* all exemplified a power of concentration which was certainly new to my ears.

A range of exemplary opera performances – many of them my actual first experience of the pieces – ranging from Gluck's *Orfeo ed Euridice* and Verdi's *Il trovatore* to Bizet's *Carmen,* meant that I could not resist the draw of returning to Salzburg year after year. With the establishment of the Easter Festival alongside the Summer one, Karajan was able to draw from his supporters an even greater commitment: a subscription guaranteed concerts, an opera and an oratorio alongside an open rehearsal and a set of LP records personally autographed. Admittedly this rather exclusive gathering did attract some psychophants, but the large part of the audience comprised serious music-lovers who returned year after year. The successful marketing strategy drew some bitter resentment from Karajan's opponents in Salzburg and elsewhere, but nowhere more vehemently than from the British critical fraternity who could grasp little that stepped beyond their own parochial experiences – after all, musical excellence in Britain's concert halls was only to be had when some eminent soloist or conductor visited from abroad.

The orchestral concerts at Salzburg's summer festivals had traditionally been the domain of the *Wiener Philharmoniker,* who had also provided most of the opera performances as well. But it was Herbert von Karajan's wish to introduce the best of the world's other orchestras, not least his own Berliners. This is an innovation which has continued right up to the present day. However, what was unique for just one decade up to the mid 1970s was the opportunity he took, whilst the Berliners were in Salzburg, to transport a small group of them for an extended "holiday" to St Moritz in Switzerland to record baroque and early classical repertoire for Deutsche Grammophon. Starting with the Brandenburg Concerti but going on to embrace the two great and opulent String Divertimenti of Mozart (K287 and K334 – for which Karajan had a special affection) but also taking in works by Handel, Vivaldi and smaller pieces by the likes of Pachelbel and Albinoni. All of this is an area of special controversy in this conductor's concert repertoire, more so nowadays since it has become the preserve of the so-called "authentic" specialists. In my view the historical approach is misguided - for me, as a listener, the standard symphony orchestra is much to be preferred, and there is certainly no lack of vitality or unanimity in Karajan's generous approach to the Handel op 6 Concerti grossi or indeed to the Mozart Symphonies.

When first recording the Mozart Divertimento K287, Karajan is reported to have used as a reference the Toscanini NBC version then current, but adding an sonority which the Italian maestro lacks. However, mention of Toscanini reminds us that he was Karajan's great inspiration when he visited Germany in the early 1930s with the La Scala opera company and first placed an opera like Donizetti's *Lucia di Lammermoor* on the North European musical map. Karajan's own recordings and stage performances of the Italian repertoire, primarily those with Maria Callas (*Madama Butterfly, Il trovatore* and *Lucia di Lammermoor)* but also later versions of *Aida, Otello* and *La boheme,* attest to a seriousness of approach so often lacking in the native Italian approach but at the same time rendering full justice to the ripe mediterranean essence of the music. Nowhere is this more fully revealed than in the various albums of opera intermezzi and ballet music set down with the Philharmonia Orchestra and later again with the Berlin Philharmonic.

Soon after Karajan's death in 1989 a centre was set up in Vienna with the purpose of preserving and promoting his legacy in sound and video formats. I was approached at the time with a view to managing this, but ultimately the position went to an Austrian national. Now that centre has transmogrified into an "institute" based appropriately in Karajan's birthplace of Salzburg. Contact has been re-established, and I am looking forward to the possibility of compiling a new discography in collaboration with the Institute. Such a discography is needed, not only in order to bring attention to newly-discovered archive material but also to highlight important restorations of the existing recorded legacy which did not always fare so well in the earliest compact disc re-issues. I refer in particular to the important EMI collaboration between Karajan and the Philharmonia Orchestra. Both mono and stereo LPs from that era are rightly prized by collectors, but the CDs which EMI started producing from the late 1980s onwards added what I would describe as an artificial glassiness (presumably the result of over-zealous digitalisation of the sound?). Fortunately Warner, who in recent years have swallowed up the old EMI recording empire, seem also to have inherited some technical staff who appreciate the original values of producer Walter Legge's sound ethos (mellowness and depth even within the confines of a monophonic sound picture), and they are now starting to re-issue the entire corpus in sound which approaches those prized originals, beginning with the cycle of Beethoven symphonies no less.

Karajan in Russia

Between 28 May and 8 June 1969 Herbert von Karajan and the Berliner Philharmoniker undertook a mini-tour of concerts in the Soviet Union, London and Paris. For both conductor and orchestra this was a third time in Russia – Karajan had been there briefly in 1962 with the Wiener Philharmoniker, and again with the company of La Scala Milan in 1964. For the Berliners, however, these appear to have been their first concerts there since appearances in 1899 and 1904 under the conductorship of Artur Nikisch.

During the 1980s the Russian state-owned record company Melodiya had published three separate LPs with works drawn from the three 1969 concerts given in the Great Hall of the Moscow Conservatory. Now they have gone a step further and issued the three programmes in their entirety.

Keen anticipation and political controversy surrounded this visit to the Soviet Union by an ensemble which was culturally representative of the Federal Republic of Germany rather than the Communist East German State, and it is reported that at least at one of the concerts an announcement had to be made to make it clear that the Orchestra was from West Berlin, a fact apparently not stated in the printed programme books. Works from the Moscow concerts were then repeated in those given in Leningrad on 1 and 2 June, and it was one of these which Shostakovich himself attended (rather than the recorded Moscow one) to hear the performance of his Tenth Symphony.

The sound quality on these CDs is of acceptable mono broadcast quality, and therefore does not rival that on commercially published versions of this core Karajan repertoire. However, the frisson of live performance more than compensates for any sonic deficiency. Bach and Mozart works are played defiantly as mainstream orchestral pieces, so will not be to the taste of baroque specialists! Where we can all agree is in the case of the Shostakovich Tenth, a performance often recalled by various other commentators and broadcasters on the strength of that rare Melodiya LP but now thankfully made available to a wider listening audience.

Wilhelm Furtwängler

There were three great musicians who I only narrowly missed experiencing in the flesh and who shared the initial F. They were the singers Kirsten Flagstad and Kathleen Ferrier and, most significantly for me, the conductor Wilhelm Furtwängler. Furtwängler had last visited London two years before I started attending concerts. It did not worry me that he possessed an extreme antipathy to his rival (and eventual successor) Herbert von Karajan – indeed I was blissfully unaware of this fact as I listened enthralled to Furtwängler's well-known LPs of the Schubert and Beethoven Ninth Symphonies. The 1960s were not a good time for mono recordings, as they had been superseded technically by stereophonic ones. Indeed, the two I have mentioned were just about the only ones of Furtwängler to survive in the catalogue.

I recall reading in the *Daily Telegraph* that plans were afoot to form a Furtwängler Society with the aim of urging the record companies to re-issue the official legacy as well as to negotiate for publication of many surviving radio broadcasts. I never actually met Paul Minchin, the Furtwängler Society's first chairman, but his successor John Baker has become a good friend, and when John resigned from the position in the mid 1970s, I was voted in as the third chairman. Minchin, who spoke no German, had rather alienated Elisabeth Furtwängler, the conductor's widow, and it was my first wish to regain Elisabeth's confidence and support for what we were trying to do. In the following years we enjoyed a number of fruitful meetings (I remember the very first one in 1979 in her Berlin hotel bedroom at the close of celebrations that had marked the twenty-fifth anniversary of the conductor's death), later again in Berlin and Paris but, most memorably, on a visit to her home at Le Basset Coulon near Montreux. That meeting had been engineered by another Society member, Jim Parsons, who had known Elisabeth since 1954, when he had attended Furtwängler's final appearances at the Salzburg Festival. Elisabeth, who more than once visited London for Furtwängler Society events under my auspices, was a personality of exceptional integrity and warmth, entirely unaffected by her connections – indeed, her only weakness was not always being able to say no to unwelcome visitors, mostly from the United States.

Opposite page: John Hunt with Elisabeth Furtwängler in Paris in 1995

Other Furtwängler Societies have come and gone - only the French one seems to remain active – reminding us that such organisations perhaps do have a limited shelf life once their purpose has been served (I can recall societies devoted to other conductors like Toscanini, Beecham and Stokowski which have subsequently ceased to exist).

Furtwängler and the Beethoven Ninth

The original HMV LP set ALP 1286-1287, containing this 1951 concert at Bayreuth's post-war reopening, still continues to fetch amazing prices on the collectors' market if it can be found in pristine condition. Until 2008 our knowledge of the concert was restricted to EMI's classic edition in its manifold incarnations. It had long been cherished by devotees in spite of the subsequent circulation of many other Furtwängler versions of the symphony drawn from between 1937 and 1954. The situation then changed with the publication of at least two versions of the 1951 performance which possess marked differences to EMI's. In brief, it emerged that EMI's recording had been taken from a dress rehearsal (*Generalprobe)* held on the morning of the concert, whereas new editions from Orfeo and the Japanese Furtwängler Centre give us the actual concert. Accusations from over-enthusiastic Japanese collectors that EMI's Walter Legge had carried out some form of deception are quite unjustified (the original HMV set had merely stated "recorded on 29 July 1951", which was correct).

Sviatoslav Richter

There remains one more pillar in my five-man pantheon of musicians, and that is the Russian master pianist Sviatoslav Richter, whose UK career I was able to follow right from its outset in 1961 until his final London appearances in the 1990s.

My closest personal encounter with him was on a Sunday afternoon in the mid 1970s, when he was due to give a solo recital in the Royal Festival Hall. Exiting from the Underground onto the concourse of Waterloo Station, where in those days there was a Post Office branch, I spotted Richter purchasing postage stamps! Richter's London agents must have been used to such erratic behaviour, whereby he would turn up with only minutes to spare before the concert's start.

Richter refused to be a specialist, and his vast recorded output contains very few complete cycles. This was not because he undervalued certain areas of a composer's output but because in all modesty he felt he had less to contribute there. Nevertheless I find his Mozart interpretations, for example, about which he himself always had reservations, to be of the highest integrity and seriousness.

Sviatoslav Richter was without doubt the catalyst for why, if pressed, I would choose only one genre of classical music for the proverbial desert island – and within that genre probably one single composer. I refer to the piano music of Franz Schubert, to whose works Richter brought a measured yet timeless serenity. The prime example is that final valedictory B flat sonata D960: so many eminent pianists seem to skate over the surface of the remarkable first movement, maybe out of a fear of being too deferential, but only Richter, in my experience, exploits the manic potential in a movement which presages the entire Romantic ethos of composers like Anton Bruckner and Hans Pfitzner.

A fine documentary film by Bruno Monsaignon releases valuable insights into the complex character of Sviatoslav Richter, and I would recommend it to every piano enthusiast.

Franz Schubert and the well of loneliness

"When I wanted to sing of love, it turned into pain; and
when I wanted to sing only of pain, it turned into love"
– Franz Schubert

In several contemporary prints Schubert is depicted as surrounded by a group of friends in convivial socialising and music-making. His profoundest music, however, paints quite a different picture: beauty becomes the channel for a long journey into the very depths of the human predicament.

As already stated, it was Sviatoslav Richter's Schubert performances which first alerted me to the power of this remarkable composer and which place him for me in the very forefront of Western cultural achievement. Indeed, if I were called on to compile a shortlist of seminal musical works, I could easily do so without straying beyond this one composer – I think not only of the late piano sonatas but equally other piano pieces, the mighty String Quintet and Great C major Symphony, not to mention the corpus of songs, both individual and cyclic.

Nearing a thousand entries in the Deutsch catalogue of Schubert's works, this makes even Mozart seem a part-timer (only around 600), but at the same time underlines the fact that only the tip of this iceberg has really achieved its deserved recognition from concert-goers and record collectors. Taking the piano works alone, there exist 13 fragmentary (incomplete) sonatas written by Schubert between the ages of 18 and 22, a second group of 5 from the ages of 26-29 and a final trilogy (D958, D959 and D960) from the year of his death at the age of 31. Yet all this is only the beginning of the instrumental catalogue, for there follow the Fantasies, Impromptus, Moments musicaux, Allegros, Andantes, Rondos, Scherzi, Marches and many more falling into the category of Klavierstücke (simply Piano pieces). Then there are over 400

Dances, many of them Ländler or Ecossaises, some of which were helped to fame by appearing in Franz Liszt's arrangements as *Soirees de Vienne.* Nor have we yet mentioned the body of works for piano duet and four hands. As far as I know, no record company has ever attempted to embrace this vast oeuvre in its entirety, and I am at least in the process of trying to catalogue them all (with mention of desirable recordings where appropriate). For it seems to me that even pioneers of Schubert playing – the likes of Edwin Fischer, Artur Schnabel, Paul Badura-Skoda or Alfred Brendel – have really only dipped their pianistic toes into this ocean of precious music. For the Schubert piano music which has so far been recorded, my preferred interpreters, either on record or in the concert hall, have been Ingrid Haebler, the East German Dieter Zechlin, the Russian Richter protégé Elisabeth Leonskaja and latterly Paul Lewis.

I have already hinted at the deep foreboding which Schubert invokes in that final Piano Sonata D960, but there are many other examples where he threatens to go off the rails, so to speak, such as in the earlier D959 Sonata (an adagio movement where tonality is momentarily lost), various moments in the incidental music to *Rosamunde* and the sublime slow movement of the String Quintet D956. Schubert's forbears were his fellow Austrians Haydn and Mozart (the latter's solo keyboard music seems to inhabit much that same world which is sad yet consoling). And after him there is a direct line on to Schumann and later Romantics like Bruckner.

Musical evenings, lecture recitals and discographies

It was after leaving EMI in 1963 and starting to work in personnel administration for the long since defunct Navy, Army and Air Force Institutes that I began organising record recitals for a group of friends and work colleagues: these continued for a good fifteen years, and it was both interesting and rewarding to see how people with no specialist interest in classical music might be persuaded to spend an hour or two listening to pieces even as advanced as Berg's *Wozzeck*!

This prompted me to plan a series of lecture recitals for music groups up and down the country (even as far as Ireland), later for the Wagner Society and the Recorded Vocal Art Society in London – by this time I was back in record retailing.

What amazed me once I had contact with the record companies again was the reluctance to fully explore their past legacies. In the case of Wilhelm Furtwängler, both EMI and Deutsche Grammophon had knowledgable people in their backrooms, and yet they seemed to regard their old recordings as some secret hoard rather than pushing for it to be marketed and made available to the modern public. The story of how the Furtwängler Society had to bully and cajole for the issue of Furtwängler's Rome *Ring* is by now well-known.

Stephen J. Pettitt had written a history of the Philharmonia Orchestra, which in 1985 was celebrating its fortieth birthday, but his publishers did not wish, for some unknown reason, to include an all-important discography in the book. This came my way and appeared as one of the first in my own series of discographies – prior to it, I had already published the first of six discographies devoted to Furtwängler (a seventh is now in the planning stage). I soon went on to cover other recording artists – conductors, singers, pianists, orchestras and even entire record labels. Always ready to help was the American scholar Michael Gray, as the discographies proved to be a useful tool for making the record companies aware of their past legacies.

The power of opera – and the curse of the "director"

Although I continue to maintain my first love to be purely instrumental music, there is no denying the powerful influence which the human voice exerts when it becomes involved in making music. However strongly one might resist, the blend of drama and song which makes up opera is hard to ignore. As will have become clear by now, my personal preference is for music of the German school, and this applies equally in the realm of opera. More about Wagner and Bayreuth later, but in the Italian field I am drawn more to the *bel canto* school (Bellini and Donizetti) and to Puccini rather than to the earthy (and sometimes rumbustious) Verdi.

Sadly in recent times the enjoyment of opera has for me been sullied by the scourge which is the interventionalist opera director, adding from his own over-active imagination to compensate for what he lacks in knowledge of a composer's intentions. Apart from my regular continental visits, I enjoyed long periods attending opera performances at Glyndebourne (my mother had worked for the John Lewis partnership and had access to tickets) and at Welsh National Opera (for many years my good friend Maisie Woodard and I attended their regular seasons at the Bristol Hippodrome). However, both these organisations seem to have sold their musical souls to the devil producers who distort and cheapen the great pieces of musical theatre. There are of course exceptions, and in recent years Welsh National Opera has offered fine renditions of *Lohengrin* and *Die Meistersinger von Nürnberg* in their splendid new home on Cardiff Bay.

I cannot really see how the fashion for extreme productions can be blamed on the German school which originated in the old German Democratic Republic with pioneers like Walter Felsenstein, Joachim Herz, Götz Friederich and Harry Kupfer. These men still had great respect for the operatic text and the guidance which this gives for bringing an opera to the stage.

In retrospect, I would count my most memorable experiences of repertory opera to have been those at Netherlands Opera (courtesy of my friend Roderick Krüsemann) and the two European houses which I have regarded as my *Stammhäuser*, Deutsche Oper Berlin

(89 performances over a period of 35 years) and Wiener Staatsoper (49 performances over 49 years).

Christian Thielemann, Pfitzner's *Palestrina* and Strauss' *Die Frau ohne Schatten*

After the death of Herbert von Karajan in 1989, I had assumed that I would enjoy a period of stocktaking and introspection as far as high quality music-making was concerned and that I would live on my memories of a golden era which for me had lasted from 1957 until the close of the 1989 Salzburg Easter Festival.

I certainly had little expectation of the major revelation which presented itself to me in 1997 when Covent Garden unveiled the first professional production in Britain of an opera which had seen the light of day exactly 80 years earlier, Hans Pfitzner's *Palestrina.* I will not go into the reasons for that delay (political correctness must have had something to do with it, as Pfitzner had associated himself with Germany's National Socialists). The shatteringly beautiful score of this romantic "musical legend", depicting the struggle of the sixteenth-century composer Giovanni Pierluigi da Palestrina to free himself from the suffocating confines of Church and State, is unashamedly Wagnerian in its tonality and breathtakingly seductive in turn. To conduct it we had a young German, Christian Thielemann, who in only just over a decade of professional activity had already established himself as a provocative upholder of the true integrity of the German musical values which manifest themselves in the works of Wagner, Bruckner and Richard Strauss as well as in the less well-charted backwaters of Pfitzner, Humperdinck, Reger, Busoni and the like. The production enjoyed such success that, as well as being revived at Covent Garden three years later, it was transferred to the Metropolitan Opera in New York (still under Thielemann's baton) and to the Deutsche Oper am Rhein in Düsseldorf.

Thielemann had also conducted a number of very successful concerts (and recordings) with the Philharmonia Orchestra, but as 1997 was the year in which I retired from my last full-time job in the Civil Service, I decided to investigate the conductor's work at Berlin's Deutsche Oper (he had become Generalmusikdirektor there at around the same time). The harvest of performances which I heard with him over the next ten years was indeed rich: all the major Wagner (with the exception of *Tannhäuser,* which I did later hear him conduct in Bayreuth), Marschner's *Hans Heiling,* Henze's *Prinz von Homburg,* Puccini's *La fanciulla del West,* Korngold's *Die tote Stadt,* Strauss' *Der Rosenkavalier* and *Daphne* and, most significantly, *Die Frau ohne Schatten,* the fairy-tale setting which Strauss and his librettist Hugo von Hofmannsthal worked on at almost the same time as Pfitzner was composing *Palestrina.* Like the latter work, its blend of compassion and Wagnerian passion fits the conducting style of Christian Thielemann like a glove.

It was the series of *Frau* perfortmances which I heard Thielemann conduct in Berlin between 1998 and 2005 and my growing obsession with the piece that inspired me to compile, with the help pf fellow enthusiast Neville Sumpter, a discography of the opera: commercial gramophone recordings of it have been few and far between, but there exists a vast reservoir of recorded broadcasts (well over 100, in fact) which we assembled and assessed. As I explained in the introduction to the book, I had been in love with the opera (and rate it above *Elektra* and *Der Rosenkavalier*) ever since hearing its British premiere in 1966 (a guest performance by the Hamburg Staatsoper in the Sadlers Wells Theatre) and, a year later, when the conductor Georg Solti introduced it to Covent Garden. Further down the line, Welsh National Opera mounted an English-language production which I rate as the finest ever in my experience (notwithstanding Salzburg Festival performances under the Strauss disciple Karl Böhm in 1974-1975).

One other aspect of my *Frau* encounters needs mentioning. When conductor Clemens Krauss had brought the opera to the Salzburg Festival in 1933, he had invited an old friend from his days at the Frankfurt Opera to come and give an introductory lecture on a piece still considered extremely difficult for the average opera-goer. This was Mita Mayer-Lismann, whose daughter Elsa was to come to Britain as a Jewish refugee and who, after the war, gained a reputation as an enthusiastic lecturer on opera as well as eventually founding a workshop training young singers in stagecraft. When I first met Elsa, herself a trained pianist and singer, she was giving introductory talks on the operas being played each year at the Glyndebourne Festival, and when Welsh National Opera brought their production of *Die Frau ohne Schatten* to London in 1981, she presented an evening of fascinating insights into the opera. Elsa's animated descriptions of the characters and situations remain with me to this day.

Bayreuth

That a modest-sized provincial town in the extreme North of Bavaria should possess such a strong individual character is down to two things. Chosen by Richard Wagner to host his own *Bühnenfestspiele* (precisely because of its comparative geographical remoteness), it is also in the heart of an historically rich region bordering on Saxony which, since German re-unification has formed itself into the *Sächsisch-Bayerisches Städtenetz* with its northerly neighbours Hof, Plauen, Zwickau (birthplace of Robert Schumann) and Chemnitz (the Communists knew that as Karl-Marx-Stadt). For the post-war visitors to the Bayreuth Festival up until 1989, this was virtually the end of the railway line which connected it to Nurnberg from the South. And that was very much part of the attraction of a visit to Bayreuth, where all one had to do before attending an afternoon performance in the Festspielhaus was to spend the earlier part of the day in one of the town's elegant parks contemplating Richard Wagner – he would certainly have approved of that!

Sadly the history of Bayreuth's Wagner associations is very much distorted by the politically correctness of modern commentators, but in my early visits to the Festival (starting in 1957) one still got glimpses of an earlier age, with Winifred Wagner, the composer's English-born daughter-in-law, still holding court to vistors in the garden of her villa adjoining the composer's own home of Wahnfried. Even Winifred's son Wolfgang, who with his brother Wieland had re-opened the Festival back in 1951, was still seen mingling with the guests before brass fanfares heralded them into the Festspielhaus. As the theatre had been purpose-built to unveil Wagner's epic cycle *Der Ring des Nibelungen,* I count myself lucky to have *Ring* performances under the direction of Rudolf Kempe, Horst Stein, Pierre Boulez, Daniel Barenboim and Christian Thielemann – and also under Thielemann a commemorative rendering of the Beethoven Ninth Symphony, which previously Wagner had conducted when laying the theatre's foundation stone, and which again Furtwängler had directed in 1951 to re-open the house after the war. Most significantly of all for me, I actually heard the legendary Hans Knappertsbusch conduct *Parsifal* – although I never saw him, as this was in the days when *Parsifal* was received in respectful silence and no curtain calls were taken by the performers.

To my complete *Ring* cycles in Bayreuth I must also add a single one of *Siegfried* in the 1990s (conducted by James Levine) when I was the guest of Elisabeth Furtwängler (ever since her husband's death she had continued to receive a contingent of tickets for the Festival).

And Wagner *Ring* cycles outside of Bayreuth? Herbert von Karajan's own production in Salzburg (1967-1970), Reginald Goodall's version for English National Opera (1970s) and most recently Christian Thielemann again in the Deutsche Oper Berlin and Daniel Barenboim at the BBC Proms - the latter benefitted greatly from being played in the producer-free zone of the Royal Albert Hall.

Dresden

Although I had fallen in love with Berlin when it was still a divided city, my acquaintanceship with the Saxon city of Dresden only started after Germany was re-united, although there were still many reminders of the old days like the ruined Frauenkirche (since rebuilt). Of the city's many cultural jewels, however, the Semperoper (a ruin since its destruction by Allied bombs in 1945) had risen again in the last decade of the Communist regime.

My strong feeling of affinity with Dresden and its cultural history was boosted when, having decided to compile a discography of its venerable orchestra the Staatskapelle, I received considerable help from a retired member of the orchestra who himself has a keen interest (and much historical knowledge) in the institution's background. Klaus Heinze and I have become good friends with a shared passion, and in the summer of 2014 he invited me to be present at some of the celebrations for the 150th anniversary of Richard Strauss' birth.

One might have thought that the 2013 Richard Wagner celebrations around the musical world would be hard to trump. Not so: in 2014 all of Germany's major musical centres were marking the anniversary of Richard the Second, as his most fervent admirers are prone to calling him.

Not the least significant events, held not only on the actual birthday (11 June) but also throughout the concert seasons 2013-2014 and 2014-2015, are those organised by the city and orchestra which the composer held most dearly: Dresden and its venerable *Staatskapelle.* This orchestra counts among its former music directors a formidable array of Strauss specialists: Ernst von Schuch, Fritz Busch, Karl Böhm, Joseph Keilberth, Rudolf Kempe, Otmar Suitner and Giuseppe Sinopoli. That tradition now appears to be in excellent hands since Christian Thielemann assumed the post in 2012.

It was of course Thielemann who presided over both the current season's final subscription concert (with the *Vier letzte Lieder* and *Alpensinfonie*) as well as the actual birthday concert (with orchestral and vocal selections from all of the nine operas which had received their premiere performances in the Saxon capital between 1901 and 1938).

This was a *Vier letzte Lieder* with a difference: placed second in the sequence of songs, well known to us since their Royal Albert Hall premiere by Flagstad and Furtwängler in 1950, was an orchestration by German composer Wolfgang Rihm of the song *Malven*, conceived at the same time as the other songs but privately bequeathed to soprano Maria Jeritza (Kiri Te Kanawa recorded this in its piano-accompanied version in the 1980s). Rihm's orchestration fitted well into the Straussian sound world. And it was also a new composition by Rihm which opened the concert: the 12-minute *Ernster Gesang* was received respectfully by the Dresden audience.

Anja Harteros was in suitably lustrous voice for the occasion, with orchestral accompaniment from Thielemann and his players on a level of which other ensembles could only dream. As for the *Alpensinfonie*, we have in the UK been spoiled in recent concert seasons with some superlative readings of the work, from Bernard Haitink and the Vienna Philharmonic in the 2012 BBC Proms season and earlier this year in the Royal Festival Hall from Lorin Maazel and the Philharmonia. Thielemann's rendering did not disappoint, with the orchestra's players, already steeped in the Dresden tradition, giving even more intensity for this very special occasion. We are here very much in the sound world of *Die Frau ohne Schatten,* and Christian Thielemann must currently be hailed as the tone poem's leading exponent: performed at this level of accomplishment, *Eine Alpensinfonie* must certainly rank with Beethoven's *Pastoral* and Debussy's *La mer* as being among music's great nature depictions.

The birthday concert on 11 June was an occasion of the utmost musical luxury, televised by Arte and presumably intended for later release on DVD. No fewer than three sopranos (the voice category for which Strauss wrote many of his finest pieces) were on the platform to give us scenes from five different operas. Christine Goerke was, as at Covent Garden earlier this season, in commanding voice in Elektra's monologue and then again in the closing scene of *Salome* (my companion at this concert, a retired member of the *Staatskapelle,* would have preferred the more virginal sound of Maria Cebotari or Christel Goltz). Then came Anja Harteros in *Mein Elemer!* from *Arabella*: a singer who at the moment can put no foot wrong, it was a pity that she had not been engaged for the title role in the opera's Salzburg performances in April of this year. The final soprano on the bill was Camilla Nylund, who seemed somewhat undserpowered in the *Zweite Brautnacht* from *Die Aegyptische Helena* (Leonie Rysanek in this part is indelible in the memories of enthusiasts of my generation). However, Nylund was much more within the part for the closing scene of *Daphne.*

Placed between the items of this operagoer's dream of a programme were orchestral showpieces from *Der Rosenkavalier* (the two waltz sequences), *Feuersnot* (the ravishing Love scene) and *Die schweigsame Frau.* As an encore, many in the audience must have been hoping for the final trio from *Der Rosenkavalier*: instead we were given a repeat of the second waltz sequence.

Christian Thielemann will, in the course of the Richard Strauss celebrations, have conducted *Elektra, Der Rosenkavalier, Arabella* and *Capriccio,* as well as a host of other vocal, orchestral and chamber works. It is to be hoped that he and his Dresden players will eventually visit the UK with some of this repertoire.

Some outstanding singers

Whilst on the subject of the human voice and in particular on the marvellous parts which Richard Strauss conceived for it, I should take stock of the performers who, apart from Elisabeth Schwarzkopf, have constantly enriched my opera and song experience. Schwarzkopf was surrounded – and she was the first to admit this – by a group of co-evals who were steeped in the same Viennese training: Irmgard Seefried, Sena Jurinac, Lisa Della Casa, Elisabeth Grümmer, Hilde Gueden, Rita Streich and Christa Ludwig were the most prominent of these. Their repertoires overlapped with that of Schwarzkopf, but sometimes extended beyond it, and I missed no opportunity of hearing them when they visited London or during my continental forays. Particularly memorable was a 1967 song recital by Grümmer in the Queen Elizabeth Hall, which included a performance of the Schumann song cycle *Frauenliebe und –leben.* This was a tradition kept very much alive for later generations by the likes of Gundula Janowitz. Margaret Price and Soile Isokoski. In the tenor department and from this same Viennese background I cannot fail to mention the ravishingly mellifluous voice of Anton Dermota. Very late in his long career he gave a Lieder recital – again from Schumann – in the Austrian town of Linz, and I eagerly made the journey from Salzburg to hear him and talk to him a little after the concert. Nicolai Gedda was a great stylist with far wider repertoire than Dermota, but for me did not possess quite the same magic. And in the field of Italian opera, I would simply make the suggestion that the concept of *The three tenors* (you all know their names) should be amplified to include *The real three tenors*: Alfredo Kraus, Franco Corelli and Carlo Bergonzi!

Maria Callas had, of course, no coevals in the accepted sense of the word, but I was once lucky enough to hear another voice which possessed a similar aura – perhaps a certain smoky wildness (if that is an acceptable definition). That was the remarkable Magda Olivero, who made hardly any commercial gramophone recordings. And then there was the inimitable Leonie Rysanek, whom I heard as Kaiserin and Marschallin (she was a Strauss specialist), Elsa, Kundry, Fidelio and – very much in Callas territory – Medea. Victoria de los Angeles, a voice of which I heard all too little in the theatre, could induce tears in the listener after only a few bars: I recommend that you test this with one of her Italian opera recordings, say *Traviata* or *Butterfly.* Nor should it be overlooked that we possessed in Britain two remarkable lyric-dramatic exponents who, for some inexplicable reason, have not been accorded the recognition they deserve: they are Pauline Tinsley (Elektra, Salome, Färberin, Kostelnicka, Abigaille, Turandot) and Josephine Barstow (Tatyana, Salome, Arabella, Leonora, Katerina Ismailova). I mention only a few of the roles I heard each of them sing in places like Oxford, Brighton and Glasgow. I would in all honesty assert that Tinsley's Salome was the finest I ever encountered (and that includes recordings by Maria Cebotari and Ljuba Welitsch), whilst it was Barstow herself, when I met her on Salzburg railway station after she had auditioned for Herbert von Karajan, who recommended that I attend one of her performances of the Shostakovich opera *Katerina Ismailova,* which she viewed as her finest stage achievement!

And then there were the Wagnerians! In the prewar years it was voices like Leider, Flagstad, Melchior, Bockelmann and Schorr who had dominated the Wagnerian scene (both in recordings and on the stages of most international opera houses), whereas for us newcomers in the 1950s and 1960s it was the triumvirate of Birgit Nilsson, Wolfgang Windgassen and Hans Hotter. In the case of the *hochdramatisch* soprano category at least, I feel that this was an unfair situation: my view is that the steely brilliance of Birgit Nilsson was far outclassed by the warmer and more rounded interpretations of the Wagner soprano parts by Astrid Varnay and Martha Mödl, let alone the wild abandon of Gwyneth Jones! One can sample Varnay in any of her live recordings as Ortrud in *Lohengrin* (this was the part with which she brought the house down when the Hamburg Staatsoper visited London's Sadlers Wells Theatre in 1962); Mödl is at her very finest in a Karajan-led *Tristan und Isolde* from Bayreuth in 1952 or a recording of the *Wesendonk-Lieder* conducted by Joseph Keilberth (we can also view her late in her career in the cameo role of the Countess in *Pique Dame,* which was televised in the 1990s). Varnay also electrified audiences in various recorded performances as Kostelnicka in Janacek's *Jenufa,* which I heard her sing both at Covent Garden and in Munich – a role in which Gwyneth Jones also made one of her last stage appearances (this I heard in Dresden).

The Proms – and some concluding words

This must be the most ambivalent, but nonetheless important, strand in my sixty years of musical experience. Only in the years of my full retirement have I become a regular, either in the season-ticket queue or latterly opting for a standing place on a daily basis.

Few other musical institutions have seen such a radical development over their 120-year history. In recent times they have become an important music festival, with visiting orchestras of the highest standard, but alongside this they present – naturally enough as it is the BBC and its licence payers who finance the concerts – the BBC regional orchestras in concerts which are often not of the same high standards, also presenting premieres of new commissions which remind me of the anecdote about the "emperor's new clothes". The Proms audience can be relied upon to applaud absolutely anything with the same untethered enthusiasm. The radio and TV concerts also now employ so-called "presenters", as opposed to mere old-fashioned announcers, who tell us, both before and after the event, what a fine rendering we have heard, arrogantly assuming that we cannot make up our own minds. Despite this there are many dedicated and sensitive music-lovers among the Proms audience, and I have even made some good friends here over the past decade.

I strongly feel that people will come to classical music of their own accord, as indeed they choose to come to any other pastime or life interest, and do not need "persuading" in the condescending manner adopted by the Radio 3 presenters (they are sometimes even unable to pronounce composers' names, to add to the general embarrassment of it all!).

Having already described my overriding passion for the piano music of Franz Schubert, I came back to such thoughts when turning on the radio randomly for *Private Passions* (a higher-level version of *Desert Island Discs)* and found that the interviewee had selected the very piece which could sum up my obsession, the *Andantino* from the Sonata D959, that view from the precipice into the depths of despair. I still have much to investigate in the piano works of Schubert's direct predecessors Haydn and Mozart or his successor Robert Schumann. Funnily enough in view of my aversion to the sound of the solo harpsichord, I recently chanced on some solo Mozart pieces played on the fortepiano by a young South African player Kristian Bezuidenhout, and found them to my liking (proving perhaps that after all I am not a complete reactionary!) My previous experience of music for the harpsichord had been limited to some transcriptions for piano by the brilliant Hungarian virtuoso György Cziffra.

Final thoughts on favourites from the operatic canon? Towering above all else is the Richard Strauss masterpiece *Die Frau ohne Schatten,* followed closely by Hans Pfitzner's *Palestrina* and Wagner's *Parsifal* and *Meistersinger.* In the case of Wagner it is probably more accurate to nominate whichever of the music dramas I have heard most recently: *Tannhäuser* and *Lohengrin* (still described by their composer as "romantic operas") come to mind as clear forerunners of *Palestrina.* And the question often arises as to why "comedies" like *Der Rosenkavalier* or *Meistersinger* should be so life-enhancing and yet possess a vein of sadness and introspection so touching to the human psyche. As for another operatic masterpiece, I am sorry to report that I left halfway through a recent performance of Mozart's *Don Giovanni* (it was set in a brothel). This musico-dramatic representation of a pivotal legend was one of many, both before and after Mozart, culminating in the famous orchestral tone poem *Don Juan* by Richard Strauss. *Don Giovanni* exists in Prague and Vienna versions, the latter dropping one of the tenor's arias as well as its finale pantomime underlining the work's moral. Only Carl Ebert and Fritz Busch, in 1930s Glyndebourne, restored these elements, yet now there is a tendency to return to that Vienna edition (Deutsche Oper Berlin 2010 and Covent Garden 2013).

Some record collectors give the impression that they have never set foot in a concert hall or opera house: for me, the two worlds of mechanical reproduction and participation in the live experience have always been inseparable, and in these brief recollections I have unashamedly mixed memories from both areas.

In the course of my random notes I have made reference to the friends and colleagues who have accompanied me, for longer or shorter durations, either stimulating me with ideas or provoking me with contrary opinions. Those not mentioned in the text I will attempt now to enumerate, in alphabetical order:-

Yasushi Aisa
Edward Allnatt
Richard Ames
Leslie Austin
Josephine Baker
Martin Bligh
Paul Bowen
Philip Chang
Lyn Clemo
Clifford Elkin
Johann Gratz
Marlen Hall
John Hancock
John Harmer
Roger Hewland
Bill Holland
John Hooper
Gordon Hutchings
David Lampon
Philippe Leduc
Sylvia Loeb
Bob Matthew-Walker
Mins Minssen
Richard Osborne
James Pearson
Aman Pedersen
Jenny Riley
James Simpson
Ian Slade
Terje Thorp
and all my discography subscribers

Books published by Travis & Emery Music Bookshop:

Anon.: Hymnarium Sarisburiense, cum Rubricis et Notis Musicis.
Anon.: Säcularfeier des Geburtstages von Ludwig van Beethoven
Agricola, Johann Friedrich from Tosi: Anleitung zur Singkunst.
Allen, Percy: The Stage Life of Mrs. Stirling: With ... C19th Theatre
Bach, C.P.E.: edited W. Emery: Nekrolog or Obituary Notice of J.S. Bach.
Bateson, Naomi Judith: Alcock of Salisbury
Bathe, William: A Briefe Introduction to the Skill of Song
Berlioz, Hector: Autobiography of Hector Berlioz, (2 vols.)
Buckley, Robert John: Sir Edward Elgar
Burney, Charles: The Present State of Music in France and Italy
Burney, Charles: The Present State of Music in Germany, The Netherlands …
Burney, Charles: Account of an Infant Musician
Burney, Charles: An Account of the Musical Performances ... Handel
Burney, Karl: Nachricht von Georg Friedrich Handel's Lebensumstanden.
Burns, Robert: The Caledonian Musical Museum .. Best Scotch Songs. (1810)
Cobbett, W.W.: Cobbett's Cyclopedic Survey of Chamber Music. (2 vols.)
Corrette, Michel: Le Maitre de Clavecin
Cox, John Edmund: Musical Recollections of the Last Half Century. (2 vols.)
Crimp, Bryan: Dear Mr. Rosenthal … Dear Mr. Gaisberg …
Crimp, Bryan: Solo: The Biography of Solomon
Crotch, William: Substance of Several Courses of Lectures on Music
d'Indy, Vincent: Beethoven: Biographie Critique
d'Indy, Vincent: Beethoven: A Critical Biography
d'Indy, Vincent: Cesar Franck (in English)
d'Indy, Vincent: César Franck (in French)
Dianna, B.A.: Benjamin Britten's Holy Theatre
Dolge, Alfred: Pianos and Their Makers. A Comprehensive History
Fischhof, Joseph: Versuch einer Geschichte des Clavierbaues. (Faksimile 1853).
Fuller-Maitland, J.A.: The Music of Parry and Stanford
Geminiani, Francesco: The Art of Playing the Violin.
Häuser: Musikalisches Lexikon. 2 vols in one.
Hawkins, John: A General History of the Science & Practice of Music (5 vols.)
Holmes, Edward: A Ramble among the Musicians of Germany
Hopkins, Antony: The Concertgoer's Companion - Bach to Haydn.
Hopkins, Antony: The Concertgoer's Companion – Holst to Webern.
Hopkins, Antony: Music All Around Me
Hopkins, Antony: Sounds of Music / Sounds of the Orchestra
Hopkins, Antony: The Nine Symphonies of Beethoven
Hopkins, Antony: Understanding Music

Books published by Travis & Emery Music Bookshop:

Hopkins, Edward & Rimboult, Edward: The Organ. Its History & Construction.
Hunt, John: - see separate list of discographies at the end of these titles
Iliffe, Frederick: The Forty-Eight Preludes and Fugues of John Sebastian Bach
Isaacs, Lewis: Hänsel and Gretel. A Guide to Humperdinck's Opera.
Isaacs, Lewis: Königskinder (Royal Children). Guide to Humperdinck's Opera.
Kastner: Manuel Général de Musique Militaire
Kenney, Charles Lamb: A Memoir of Michael William Balfe
Klein, Hermann: Thirty years of musical Life in London, 1870-1900
Lacassagne, M. l'Abbé Joseph : Traité Général des élémens du Chant
Lascelles (née Catley), Anne: The Life of Miss Anne Catley.
McCormack, John: John McCormack: His Own Life Story.
Mainwaring, John: Memoirs of the Life of the Late George Frederic Handel
Malcolm, Alexander: A Treaty of Music: Speculative, Practical and Historical
Manshardt, Thomas: Aspects of Cortot
Marx, Adolph Bernhard: Die Kunst des Gesanges, Theoretisch-Practisch
May, Florence: The Life of Brahms
May, Florence: The Girlhood Of Clara Schumann: Clara Wieck And Her Time.
Mellers, Wilfrid: Angels of the Night: Popular Female Singers of Our Time
Mellers, Wilfrid: Bach and the Dance of God
Mellers, Wilfrid: Beethoven and the Voice of God
Mellers, Wilfrid: Caliban Reborn - Renewal in Twentieth Century Music
Mellers, Wilfrid: Darker Shade of Pale, A Backdrop to Bob Dylan
Mellers, Wilfrid: François Couperin and the French Classical Tradition
Mellers, Wilfrid: Harmonious Meeting
Mellers, Wilfrid: Le Jardin Retrouvé, The Music of Frederic Mompou
Mellers, Wilfrid: Music and Society, England and the European Tradition
Mellers, Wilfrid: Music in a New Found Land: ... ... American Music
Mellers, Wilfrid: Romanticism and the Twentieth Century (from 1800)
Mellers, Wilfrid: The Masks of Orpheus: ...... the Story of European Music.
Mellers, Wilfrid: The Sonata Principle (from c. 1750)
Mellers, Wilfrid: Vaughan Williams and the Vision of Albion
Newmarch, Rosa: Henry J. Wood
Newmarch, Rosa: Jean Sibelius
Newmarch, Rosa: Mary Wakefield, a Memoir
Newmarch, Rosa: The Concert-Goer's Library
Newmarch, Rosa: The Music of Czechoslovakia
Newmarch, Rosa: The Russian Opera.
Nicholas, Jeremy: Godowsky, the Pianists' Pianist
Niecks, Frederick: The Life oc Chopin. (2 vols.)
Panchianio, Cattuffio: Rutzvanscad Il Giovine

Books published by Travis & Emery Music Bookshop:

Pearce, Charles: Sims Reeves, Fifty Years of Music in England.
Pepusch, John Christopher: A Treatise on Harmony ...
Pettitt, Stephen: Philharmonia Orchestra: A Record of Achievement, 1948-1985
Pettitt, Stephen (ed. Hunt): Philharmonia Orchestra: Discography 1945-1987
Playford, John: An Introduction to the Skill of Musick.
Porte, John: Sir Charles Villiers Stanford.
Quantz, Johann: Versuch einer Anweisung die Flöte traversiere zu spielen.
Rameau, Jean-Philippe: Code de Musique Pratique, ou Methodes.
Rameau, Jean-Philippe: Erreurs sur La Musique dans l'Encyclopédie
Rastall, Richard: The Notation of Western Music.
Rimbault, Edward: The Pianoforte, Its Origins, Progress, and Construction.
Rousseau, Jean Jacques: Dictionnaire de Musique
Rubinstein, Anton : Guide to the proper use of the Pianoforte Pedals.
Sainsbury, John S.: Dictionary of Musicians. (1825). (2 vols.)
Schumann, Clara & Brahms, Johannes: Letters 1853-1896. (2 vols.)
Scott-Sutherland: Arnold Bax
Serré de Rieux, Jean de : Les dons des Enfans de Latone
Simpson, Christopher: A Compendium of Practical Musick in Five Parts
Smyth, Ethel: Impressions That Remained. (2 vols.)
Spohr, Louis: Autobiography
Spohr, Louis: Grand Violin School
Tans'ur, William: A New Musical Grammar; or The Harmonical Spectator
Terry, Charles Sanford: Bach's Chorals – Parts 1, 2 and 3.
Terry, Charles Sanford: John Christian Bach
Terry, Charles Sanford: J.S. Bach's Original Hymn-Tunes - Congregational Use.
Terry, Charles Sanford: Four-Part Chorals of J.S. Bach. (German & English)
Terry, Charles Sanford: Joh. Seb. Bach, Cantata Texts, Sacred and Secular.
Terry, Charles Sanford: The Origins of the Family of Bach Musicians.
Tosi, Pierfrancesco: Opinioni de' Cantori Antichi, e Moderni
Tosi, Pierfrancesco: Observations on the Florid Song.
Tovey, Donald Francis: A Musician Talks, The Integrity of Music
Tovey, Donald Francis: A Musician Talks, Musical Textures
Tovey, Donald Francis: A Companion to "The Art of the Fugue" J.S. Bach
Tovey, Donald Francis: A Companion to Beethoven's Pianoforte Sonatas
Tovey, Donald Francis: Beethoven
Tovey, Donald Francis: Essays in Musical Analysis. (6 vols.).
Tovey, Donald Francis: The integrity of music
Tovey, Donald Francis: Musical Textures

Books published by Travis & Emery Music Bookshop:

Tovey, Donald Francis: Some English Symphonists
Tovey, Donald Francis: The Main Stream of Music.
Van der Straeten, Edmund: History of the Violoncello, The Viol da Gamba …
Van der Straeten, Edmund: History of the Violin, Its Ancestors… (2 vols.)
Walther, J. G. [Waltern]: Musicalisches Lexikon [Musikalisches Lexicon]
Wagner, Richard: Beethoven (Leipzig 1870)
Wagner, Richard: Lebens-Bericht (Leipzig 1884)
Wagner, Richard: The Musaic of the Future (Translated by E. Dannreuther).
Wyndham, Henry Saxe: The Annals of Covent Garden Theatre. (2 vols.)
Zwirn, Gerald: Stranded Stories From The Operas

Books Distributed by Travis & Emery Music Bookshop:

Herbert-Caesari, Edgar: The Alchemy of Voice

Music published by Travis & Emery Music Bookshop:

Bach, Johann Sebastian: Sacred Songs for SCTB, arranged by Franz Wullner.
Bax, Arnold: Symphony #5, Arranged for Piano Four Hands by Walter Emery
Beranger, Pierre Jean de: Musique Des Chansons de Beranger: Airs Notes ...
Bizet, Georges: Djamileh. Vocal Score.
Donizetti, Gaetano: Betly. Dramma Giocoso in Due Atti. Vocal Score.
Frescobaldi, Girolamo: D'Arie Musicali per Cantarsi. Primo & Secondo Libro.
Handel, Purcell, Boyce, Greene ... Calliope or English Harmony: Volume First.
Hopkins, Antony: Sonatine
Purcell, Henry et al: Harmonia Sacra … The First Book, (1726)
Purcell, Henry et al: Harmonia Sacra … Book II (1726)
Sullivan, Arthur Seymour: Ivanhoe. Vocal score.
Sullivan, Arthur Seymour: The Rose of Persia. Vocal Score.
Weckerlin, Jean-Baptiste: Chansons Populaires du Pays de France

Other Books, not on Music:

Anon: A Collection of Testimonies Concerning Several Ministers of the Gospel Amongst People called Quakers, Deceased. [Facsimile of 1760 edn.].
Sandeman-Allen, Arthur: Bee-keeping with Twenty hives.

Available from: Travis & Emery at 17 Cecil Court, London, UK.
(+44) (0) 20 7 240 2129. email on sales@travis-and-emery.com .

Discographies by John Hunt.

3 Italian Conductors and 7 Viennese Sopranos: 10 Discographies: Arturo Toscanini, Guido Cantelli, Carlo Maria Giulini, Elisabeth Schwarzkopf, Irmgard Seefried, Elisabeth Gruemmer, Sena Jurinac, Hilde Gueden, Lisa Della Casa, Rita Streich.

A Gallic Trio: 3 Discographies: Charles Muench, Paul Paray, Pierre Monteux.

A Notable Quartet: 4 Discographies: Gundula Janowitz, Christa Ludwig, Nicolai Gedda, Dietrich Fischer-Dieskau.

American Classics: The Discographies of Leonard Bernstein & Eugene Ormand

Antal Dorati 1906-1988: Discography and Concert Register.

Austro-Hungarian Pianists, Discographies of Lili Kraus, Friedrich Gulda, Ingrid Haebler

Back From The Shadows: 4 Discographies: Willem Mengelberg, Dimitri Mitropoulos, Hermann Abendroth, Eduard Van Beinum.

Carlo Maria Giulini: Discography and Concert Register.

Columbia 33CX Label Discography.

Concert Hall Discography: Concert Hall Society and Concert Hall Record Club

Conductors On The Yellow Label: 8 Discographies: Fritz Lehmann, Ferdinand Leitner, Ferenc Fricsay, Eugen Jochum, Leopold Ludwig, Artur Rother, Franz Konwitschny, Igor Markevitch.

Dirigenten der DDR: Conductors of the German Democratic Republic

From Adam to Webern: the Recordings of von Karajan.

Frosh: Discography of the Richard Strauss Opera Die Frau ohne Schatten

Giants of the Keyboard: 6 Discographies: Wilhelm Kempff, Walter Gieseking, Edwin Fischer, Clara Haskil, Wilhelm Backhaus, Artur Schnabel.

Gramophone Stalwarts: 3 Separate Discographies: Bruno Walter, Erich Leinsdorf, Georg Solti.

Great Violinists: 3 Discographies: David Oistrakh, Wolfgang Schneiderhan, Arthur Grumiaux.

Hans Knappertsbusch: Kna: Concert Register and Discography of Hans Knappertsbusch, 1888-1965. Second Edition.

Her Master's Voice: Concert Register and Discography of Dame Elisabeth Schwarzkopf [Third Edition].

Hungarians in Exile: 3 Discographies: Fritz Reiner, Antal Dorati, George Szell.

Leopold Stokowski (1882-1977): Discography and Concert Register

Leopold Stokowski: Discography and Concert Listing.

Leopold Stokowski: Second Edition of the Discography.

Makers of the Philharmonia: 11 Discographies Alceo Galliera, Walter Susskind, Paul Kletzki, Nicolai Malko, Issay Dobrowen, Lovro Von Matacic, Efrem Kurtz, Otto Ackermann, Anatole Fistoulari, George Weldon, Robert Irving.

Metropolitan Sopranos: 4 Discographies: Rosa Ponselle, Eleanor Steber, Zinka Milanov, Leontyne Price.

Mezzo and Contraltos: 5 Discographies: Janet Baker, Margarete Klose, Kathleen Ferrier, Giulietta Simionato, Elisabeth Hoengen.

Mid-Century Conductors and More Viennese Singers: 10 Discographies: Karl Boehm, Victor De Sabata, Hans Knappertsbusch, Tullio Serafin, Clemens Krauss, Anton Dermota, Leonie Rysanek, Eberhard Waechter, Maria Reining, Erich Kunz.
More 20th Century Conductors: 7 Discographies: Eugen Jochum, Ferenc Fricsay, Carl Schuricht, Felix Weingartner, Josef Krips, Otto Klemperer, Erich Kleiber.
More Giants of the Keyboard: 5 Discographies: Claudio Arrau, Gyorgy Cziffra, Vladimir Horowitz, Dinu Lipatti, Artur Rubinstein.
More Musical Knights: 4 Discographies: Hamilton Harty, Charles Mackerras, Simon Rattle, John Pritchard.
Musical Knights: 6 Discographies: Henry Wood, Thomas Beecham, Adrian Boult, John Barbirolli, Reginald Goodall, Malcolm Sargent.
Philharmonic Autocrat 1: Discography of: Herbert Von Karajan [Third Edition]
Philharmonic Autocrat 2: Concert Register of Herbert Von Karajan Second Ed.
Philips Minigroove: Second Extended Version of the European Discography.
Pianists For The Connoisseur: 6 Discographies: Arturo Benedetti Michelangeli, Alfred Cortot, Alexis Weissenberg, Clifford Curzon, Solomon, Elly Ney.
Sächsische Staatskapelle Dresden: Complete Discography.
Singers of the Third Reich: 5 Discographies: Helge Roswaenge, Tiana Lemnitz, Franz Voelker, Maria Mueller, Max Lorenz.
Singers on the Yellow Label: 7 Discographies: Maria Stader, Elfriede Troetschel, Annelies Kupper, Wolfgang Windgassen, Ernst Haefliger, Josef Greindl, Kim Borg
Six Wagnerian Sopranos: 6 Discographies: Frieda Leider, Kirsten Flagstad, Astrid Varnay, Martha Moedl, Birgit Nilsson, Gwyneth Jones.
Staatskapelle Berlin. The shellac era 1916-1962.
Sviatoslav Richter: Pianist of the Century: Discography.
Teachers and Pupils: 7 Discographies: Elisabeth Schwarzkopf, Maria Ivoguen, Maria Cebotari, Meta Seinemeyer, Ljuba Welitsch, Rita Streich, Erna Berger
Tenors in a Lyric Tradition: 3 Discographies: Peter Anders, Walther Ludwig, Fritz Wunderlich.
The Art of the Diva: 3 Discographies: Claudia Muzio, Maria Callas, Magda Olivero.
The Furtwaengler Sound Sixth Edition: Discography and Concert Listing.
The Great Dictators: 3 Discographies: Evgeny Mravinsky, Artur Rodzinski, Sergiu Celibidache.
The Lyric Baritone: 5 Discographies: Hans Reinmar, Gerhard Huesch, Josef Metternich, Hermann Uhde, Eberhard Waechter.
The Post-War German Tradition: 5 Discographies: Rudolf Kempe, Joseph Keilberth, Wolfgang Sawallisch, Rafael Kubelik, Andre Cluytens.
Wagner Im Festspielhaus: Discography of the Bayreuth Festival.
Wiener Philharmoniker 1 - Vienna Philharmonic and Vienna State Opera Orchestras: Discography Part 1 1905-1954.
Wiener Philharmoniker 2 - Vienna Philharmonic and Vienna State Opera Orchestras: Discography Part 2 1954-1989.

Available from: Travis & Emery at 17 Cecil Court, London, UK.
(+44) (0) 20 7 240 2129. email on sales@travis-and-emery.com .

www.ingramcontent.com/pod-product-compliance
Ingram Content Group UK Ltd.
Pitfield, Milton Keynes, MK11 3LW, UK
UKHW020244250726
13967UKWH00004B/1514

9 781901 395297